MENTOR
& ME

How I Closed 106 Deals
My First Year in Real Estate

Alan Stewart

Dear Chris —
Here's wishing you and yours
all the best!! Sincerely! Alan —

Published by Prominence Publishing.
For information visit www.prominencepublishing.com

For more information, contact Alan Stewart at:
www.alanstewart.ca or 604-740-2353

Cover photo by Paola Stewart.

ISBN: 978-0-9737453-6-8

ACKNOWLEDGEMENTS

I'm not a full time author, and as a result, it's taken nearly five years to bring this book to publication. While the majority of the book was written in the summer of 2012, the process of finishing and the challenge of deciding when it was "done" was a daunting task.

As the title 'Mentor and Me' suggests, it's only natural that I acknowledge the impact of my real estate mentor, Ryan Campbell. While Ryan tragically passed away late in 2014 from complications suffered after contracting malaria, his legacy lives on in people like me, as well as in his wife Sue, his children Rod, Craig and Kim, and his beautiful grandchildren.

While this book is based on lessons learned from Ryan, I've also attributed many of the lessons I have learned from others and through personal experience to him. I've done so in an attempt to build a heroic character that any Realtor would look up to. Like all of us, Ryan had his flaws, but at his core what set him apart was his sincere interest in other people. It was my privilege to deliver the eulogy at Ryan's funeral and share what he meant to me. His impact on my life will never be forgotten.

Like Ryan's "too good to be true" character, my character in the book draws from the skills and talents of many. Early on in my career I surrounded myself with great people. My business partner Dave Milligan was a central figure in our success. I've witnessed a lot of real estate partnerships implode, but Dave had my best interests at heart, and I his. We were brothers in business and any success I achieved was in no small part attributable to him.

Over the years our other team members included Sue Campbell, Connie Sutherland, Diane Knight, Suzanne Jorgensen, Jean Pate and Kerry Milligan.

I continued to sell real estate until 2011, when I was licensed as a Managing Broker and began to teach what I had learned with others. I continued managing until the summer of 2016 when I returned to my career in selling real estate on the Sunshine Coast. During my time in managing I learned a multitude of lessons which have been incorporated into this book.

David Oldham saw potential in me that I hadn't seen in myself, and more importantly encouraged me to take on a new challenge. Sharon Warner, Geoff White, Ron Hamer-Jackson, Grant Gardner, Donna Pinkowski, Joe Lloyd and Phil Horth all believed in me and took up the flag for me in advancing my career. Fred Brown taught me how a sense of humour can lend itself beautifully to business. Joe Lloyd always challenged me to do the right thing.

When our company was acquired by Royal LePage in 2014 I had the opportunity to learn from new bosses, colleagues and friends. President Phil Soper reinforced my belief in the power of building relationships through empathy and understanding. He also reinforced my belief that true leaders can best express themselves and develop influence in the trenches with their troops. Gino Romanese taught me the importance of listening carefully, digesting what is being said 'between the lines,' and developing a sound plan of action. Everyone on staff that I worked with at Royal LePage, from Managing Brokers to the National Advisory Council, taught me that the real reward in life comes through helping others.

I've also watched the best of the best salespeople at work and I've paid attention to the lessons they've shared. Lance and Wendy Phillips shared the importance of family and humility. Susan Lee taught me the value of respect and reciprocity. Iain "Ironman" Edmonds inspired me to take on physical challenges in order to keep the fire within burning bright. Jasmine Botto shared how important it was to love your clients and your company. Ali Khan was a testament to the power of kindness and tenacity. Jon McRae taught me the value of 'plying one's hobby' and loving what you do for a living. Joel O'Reilly and Denise Brynelsen taught me about the importance of listing dominance and relationships and niche marketing. John McKenzie taught me about the power of being perpetually 'present' in your community. Jason Soprovich taught me about the importance of protecting your reputation by walking the walk. John Jennings taught me about being accountable to yourself and sharing responsibility with others. Sadru Mita, Marc Haslam, Rina Brown and Judy White taught me the value of taking pride in your profession and giving back to the industry.

I've learned real estate lessons from so many of the Realtors and Managers who surrounded me over the years and want to thank anyone I've ever been on the other side of a transaction with. I consider my colleagues and my competitors my friends, and I'm proud to work in an environment where there is so much mutual respect.

Others from outside of the industry have also played a part in my success and encouraged me in ways they likely aren't aware. Gord and Deb Smith and Don and Geri Stephen, our closest family friends, have always believed in me and provided my family with opportunities and kindness beyond repayment. Pat and Vicki Hazelwood and Barclay and Mary Mayo have offered spiritual guidance and direction that changed my life. Max Kretschmer and Ian and Nancy Mackay have taught me about loving your community and taking action for the benefit of others. And all my Rotarian friends have taught me about putting service above self.

My coach, Leah Goard, taught me about self belief, organization, resilience, and the power of networking with great people. Suzanne Doyle-Ingram, my publisher, who knew what I needed to know and for helping me across the finish line.

Finally, this book wouldn't have been possible without the encouragement of my family.

My greatest mentor in life was my father, Bill Stewart, who passed away only a few months after Ryan. My life was suddenly void of the input of two of the most important characters in it. It was then that I realized the importance of finishing this book and sharing it with others. I wanted to pass on some of the lessons I've learned from two great men when it came to building relationships and caring for, and listening to, others.

My sister Jill Stewart, a Calgary based Realtor, was my test reader and one of the first to lay eyes on the book. My mother Alison, a retired elementary school teacher, offered to proof read my first draft and made many important suggestions to the finished product. You have both helped me believe the book could have a positive impact on others and that pushed me to finish.

And most importantly, thank you to my wife Paola who provided unfailing support and encouragement and who allowed me the time to sit and write, without interruption, during family vacations and time at the cabin. My "headphone and laptop" time also affected my daughters, Makenzie, Samantha and Hannah, who not only waited patiently for me to finish up a chapter so that we could go exploring or cliff jumping together, but they were all incredibly supportive and understood how much the process meant to me. You four ladies are my light and inspiration and I love you all!

Table of Contents

CHAPTER ONE

GETTING STARTED

I was struggling. At the age of 36, with a wife and three young daughters at home, I was chasing a long-time dream of running my own woodworking business but instead I had pulled my family into what felt like an inescapable pit of debt. My lack of experience in the business reinforced my lack of confidence, so I was pricing jobs too low in hopes of undercutting my competition to "buy" the work away from them. My lack of skills meant costly mistakes. My devotion to my employees meant that I had delayed the inevitable and I was paying them with money I didn't have.

How did I get here? How did pursuing my dream turn into a nightmare?

It all started 3 years earlier when I volunteered to build a set of bookcases for our local church.

"Alan... these are spectacular!" said Ryan Campbell, a local Realtor® and respected member of the congregation. "I didn't know you were so talented! Have you ever thought about doing this for a living?"

"Thanks," I replied, "I've always loved woodworking, but don't often have the time to do it."

"Well, listen," he said, pulling me aside from the group. "I have a little cabinet shop listed for sale and I think you might be able to make a real go of it! The guy who's selling has told me to share that he is very motivated and I think you could negotiate a very good price for the tools, the van and all his clients. It would be a turn-key business where you could do something you love for a living."

There have been a few times in my life where I've 'vibrated' about an idea - where it just resonated with me and I felt almost helpless but to pursue it. This was one of those times. Without doing any market research and with very little planning, I decided to take a leap of faith and borrow the money from my parents to make the purchase. The $30,000 price we agreed to was significantly below what was being asked for the business and was, I thought, a fair price for the tools and materials... let alone his client list and training.

I spent the better part of a month working alongside the cabinet maker, getting a handle on his business and learning his techniques. He had systematized much of the cabinet making process and had much of it down to a science. He had been operating out of his home workshop, running as a one man show... small, fat and happy. He warned me to watch my overhead. "Don't try and be big... just be happy." But because I intended to maintain my current job, at a reduced schedule, and because of my intention to be more successful than he had been, I ignored his advice. I hired a couple of guys I knew to come and work for me and rented a storefront in our small town with our workshop in the back.

Three years later, after countless sleepless nights, I was doing my best to keep my head above water. Like an addict hitting rock bottom, I finally came to the realization that this was an unwinnable war and that there was no way for me, with my limited skills and experience, to be successful in such a small market. While it nearly killed me to admit it, I knew I was going to fail.

The embarrassment that came along with this admission was painful. I had spent years telling people how great the business was doing, hoping they would call me when they were renovating a kitchen or bathroom. At the very least I hoped that they would share a good word about me to their friends. But it had been a sham.

While I loved running the business (organizing the storefront, systematizing the workload and equipment in the back, buying inventory, taking on consignment pieces from local artists and craftspeople) I had neglected to focus on the core of my business: getting new clients and producing cabinets. I had been distracted... likely because I didn't KNOW my business. Looking back on it, regardless of how great a cabinet maker I may have been, my fate was doomed as a result of not knowing the trade and understanding what my business was.

Fate

In the last year of operation, I was contacted by the same real estate agent that had initially sold me the business, Ryan Campbell. He and his wife, Sue, were building a new house and whether out of respect as a past client or because he trusted me, he called and asked me to build his kitchens and bathrooms. We did an admirable job and they were both thrilled with the end product. Our relationship deepened as a result of his support for me and the time that he and I were able to work together in planning out the project and delivering the final product.

I was grateful for his loyalty and the fact that he didn't call any other contractors for ideas of pricing - for trusting in me. Soon after I finished that job, I closed my business for good.

It wasn't long after shutting down the cabinet making business, on a day that I was in a pretty deep depression, that I received a call from Ryan. It was a call that would change my life. Instead of hiding from me, knowing that by selling me the business he played a role in my failure, he invited me to come and work with him as his "Buyer's Agent" in his real estate practice. He offered to pay for my real estate licensing course and pay me a percentage of the deals I was able to put together from the leads he would give me, all the while mentoring me and allowing me to gain a better understanding of the business he had been so successful in for over 12 years.

I will always wonder whether or not there was any guilt in his decision to bring me into the business, but I chose to believe his explanation that he saw potential for me in the real estate business and an exit strategy for him.

Unlike most high school and university courses I had taken, where I had often muddled through the content uninterested, I devoured the Real Estate Licensing Course and three months after starting the correspondence content I was ready to write the exam. Before travelling to the University of British Columbia for the exam I remember telling my wife, "Regardless of whether I pass or fail, I'm so happy for everything I've learned. I really like this stuff and I know I'm better prepared for a lot of things in my own life now."

I whizzed through the exam in under an hour of the three hours available and scored nearly 90%. It felt really good to have mastered the course content, and doing so well gave me even more courage when I headed out with the buyers that Ryan would assign to me. It was only a matter of days after writing the exam that I received my results and submitted my license application. I was a Realtor®... and I was proud of it.

Getting To Work

While we worked for a Brokerage with an office in town, Ryan chose to work from a small detached office located on his oceanfront property. He met me in the driveway on my first day at work and after a strong handshake and some welcoming words, we walked towards the small and well kept building.

"I learned something early on in my real estate career," he said. "The only people in my life that aren't prospects are my colleagues, and I decided early on that I want to spend as much time as possible with prospects, and that's why we work here."

"But in my real estate course there was lots of talk about how important it is to get to know your colleagues, build relationships with them, and maybe even pick up some open houses or referrals from the successful ones. Isn't there a risk in being isolated from them?" I questioned.

"I guess a lot depends on the person and how self disciplined and focused they are," he said, pausing for a second. "Most Realtors® are social animals, and while I attend every sales meeting, training session and social event in the office, my experience was that the folks hanging around the office all the time were simply a distraction to me getting to work and focusing on the one thing that drives our business. If I had it to do over again, and didn't have this place to work from, I would go to the office every morning, check my mail, touch base with my broker, make my calls and then get back to the business of generating leads and helping clients."

"And how do you generate leads so that you have clients to help?" I asked, hoping for a silver bullet answer.

"That, my boy," he laughed, "is what I hope to teach you. If you focus all your working hours on helping existing clients and generating leads… you'll go a far in this business. And you can take that to the bank."

Ryan opened the door to the office and held it for me as I walked into a space that would become very familiar to me and in which I would learn lessons that would shape my future in so many ways.

Ryan and I shared the space with his wife, Sue, who maintained his website and prepared his marketing material, and his Unlicensed Assistant, Kim, who handled much of the paperwork processing and incoming leads from the internet.

The office was nicely appointed with built in workstations, a meeting desk with four chairs, high end colour laser printers, filing cabinets and a coffee area. In the back was a storage room with all the maps and information the team might need to gather information about properties in the area. It was obvious that he had invested in all the tools he required to do the job as a professional.

On my first day at work I realized that I could have an impact on the team with my aptitude for technology. One of the things that Sue was responsible for was completing and submitting paperwork to the Real Estate Board. As Ryan wanted me to learn all aspects of the business, one of my first responsibilities was to step into each role for a period of time. I sat at the computer terminal with Sue watching over my shoulder as I transcribed the property write up that my Ryan had prepared on a handwritten form.

Once I completed the write up, knowing that I would have to put the same paragraph into a brochure we would be preparing, I highlighted the paragraph by clicking and dragging my mouse across it and hit the "CTRL + C" key simultaneously. I did it so naturally that Sue didn't notice me doing it.

After we finished that form we started in on the brochure. I clicked in the field for the write up and hit "CTRL + V", the keyboard shortcut for paste, and the paragraph magically appeared in the empty space.

"What did you do?!" She exclaimed.

"What do you mean?" I asked.

"How did you do that? How did you get the write up into that space?"

"I pasted it there," I said with a smirk... assuming she was playing a practical joke on me. Realizing she wasn't kidding, I continued, "Like this." I deleted the write up and then hit the same key sequence, replacing the paragraph.

She ran across the room and grabbed Kim by the shoulder. "Come here! You have to see this."

I assumed that the Assistant, paid to input data, would have known this basic shortcut and likely would have laughed at the tip. But after I once again deleted the paragraph and pasted it back in, her mouth dropped open and she asked, "Alan, can you do the same thing on our website? We have to put it there too."

To me, COPY and PASTE were not exactly cutting edge technology. I realized then that while we often doubt ourselves, particularly in a new role, we all too often overestimate other people. We are all struggling to do the best we can, but we often miss valuable opportunities to share and add value to others by working alongside them.

(See Appendix A: Keyboard Shortcuts for REALTORS®)

I realized on my first day that I had lots to learn, but that I also had lots to offer. I committed to sharing everything I could with the people around me while learning everything I could from them that would help me build a remarkable career. Ryan and his team had a recipe for success that I wanted to be able to take advantage of for the rest of my life.

Attributes of Success: Acting like a Professional

As an Engineer with a Navy background, Ryan took every job seriously and like me he was proud of his career in real estate. He took steps to ensure his clients saw him in the same light as he saw himself by acting appropriately at all times and surrounding himself with professional people in a professional environment. Not only were we expected to dress appropriately, even though we worked in a home office, he insisted that the radio be left on in the background, set to a classical radio station to help elevate the "tone" of our workplace. For a small town home office, it was obvious that this operation was meant to run as a business, not a hobby.

Ryan expected us all to be at work at 8:30 a.m. and work a full day. "You will hear a lot of people say that this is a relationship business Alan," he'd say, "but while the job offers a lot of flexibility and fun, if you don't treat it like a business, you're doomed to fail. The 'relationships' you build are founded on acting like a professional and treating your practice as a 'business.'"

He reminded himself, and me, of our responsibilities by hanging a framed newspaper job posting for a Realtor above our filing cabinet, along with his own note in red:

REAL ESTATE SALES PROFESSIONAL JOB POSTING:

Responsibilities

- Provide guidance and assist sellers and buyers in marketing/purchasing property for the right price under the best terms
- Determine clients' needs and financial abilities in order to propose solutions that suit them
- Intermediate negotiation processes, consult clients on market conditions, prices, mortgages, legal requirements and related matters to their benefit and ensure a fair and honest dealing
- Perform comparative market analysis to assist clients in coming to terms with a property's value
- Display and market real property to possible buyers
- Prepare necessary paperwork (contracts, leases, closing statements, etc.)
- Manage transactions and exchanges
- Cooperate with appraisers, conveyancers, lawyers, notaries, lenders and home inspectors
- Develop networks and cooperate with attorneys, mortgage lenders and contractors
- Promote sales through advertisements, open houses and listing services
- Remain knowledgeable about real estate markets and best practices

...AND GENERATE LEADS!

My mentor Ryan understood and always remembered that without leads that led to clients, nothing else mattered.

One of things that struck me about Ryan was his willingness to open his home to clients and prospects. He ingratiated himself with people by offering them a level of hospitality rarely seen in our society. People found it hard to refuse him too.

I could tell that clients were often uncomfortable about being a burden to Ryan or his family by coming over for dinner after an afternoon of touring houses, but he was relentless in his invitations, rarely accepting "no" for an answer.

Ryan had no problem blending the line between clients and friends, particularly for those people that he liked or took an interest in. And by taking care of his clients as his friends, he quickly built long standing relationships with countless people. I'm convinced that Ryan truly valued other people's company and the things he could learn and share when they were together. But one of the key things that enabled him to be so gracious and hospitable was his wife.

Sue often laughed about the fact that she needed to have extra dinner prepared because she never knew when she would get a phone call from Ryan telling her that they had company coming over. And when clients, colleagues or employees went for dinner at their house, they left feeling like family. You couldn't escape a second helping of Sue's homemade dessert and you would have had to have done something offensive during dinner not to get a hug or a kiss from her when leaving. My kids even started to refer to the pair as their third set of grandparents. Relationships are everything.

"Ryan," I asked one morning after we had accepted a late invitation to join them for a barbeque the night before, "I understand that it's good for business, but doesn't Sue ever get tired of you bringing people home for dinner?"

He smiled and laughed a little. "From time to time," he said. But we agreed years ago that we would share in all our blessings with as many people as we could. We've been very fortunate and we do what we can to show our appreciation."

"But the people you entertain don't need a handout or a meal? They are usually people who have lots of money."

"They might have lots of money, but when people are looking to buy a home in our community, that often means that they are separated from their own community and family," he responded, "and that means that they may be lonely. It doesn't matter how much money you have, there's always room for a little company in your life!"

"I guess so, but don't you get tired of it?"

"Do you get tired of hanging out with me?" he asked.

"No, but I've got lots to learn from you!" I said with a laugh.

"Well it's the same for me. I've got lots to learn from you... and lots to learn from all the people we entertain." He paused... "And if I can offer a little something of value into their lives, so much the better."

A few weeks later, we were driving back to the office from a meeting when we came upon a scruffy hitchhiker with a cardboard sign that told us his destination. I kept my eyes on the road, having passed the same person countless times before, and knowing that he wasn't completely stable mentally.

"Aren't you going to pick him up?" asked Ryan.

"I hadn't planned on it."

"Come on," he pleaded. "He's a nice guy who could use a little help."

I pulled the car over as quickly as I could, but at least 40 yards past where the hitchhiker was standing.

"He doesn't have any way to get back and forth from the grocery store to his house," Ryan told me. "He and his wife are both schizophrenic, so don't take anything he says too personally."

The back door opened and the hitchhiker stuck his head in. "Heading North?" he asked.

"You bet. Get in," I said.

He put his body in first and then put his backpack on the floor between his legs, his body odour and foul breath instantly overwhelming the car. I rolled down my window an inch or so, and we started driving.

"Hi Jack," Ryan said turning back to him with a smile.

"Oh, hey Ryan!" he said, surprised. "I didn't know that was you! Who's your friend?"

"Jack, this is Alan Stewart. He works with me in the real estate business."

"Hi Jack," I offered, less than enthusiastically.

"Hi Alan," he replied. "Any friend of Ryan's is a friend of mine."

We travelled the highway together for 20 minutes with Jack sharing stories about the Schizophrenia support group he and his wife were spearheading for virtually the entire trip. "We have roast beef and Yorkshire Pudding every Tuesday night for everyone. You should come some time Alan."

Ryan winked at me.

I thanked him for the offer, but graciously declined. We pulled the car over to let Jack out at his house on the highway, his wife waiting for him on the porch. He thanked me for the ride and reached over to shake Ryan's hand.

"Thanks for getting him to stop, Ryan. I always appreciate your help."

When I lay in bed that night, reflecting on the day, I realized that one of the things that differentiated Ryan from others was the fact that he did the right things for the right reasons. While someone could have easily interpreted Ryan's actions and hospitality as self serving, what made people respond to him was that he was completely sincere. He had a heart for taking care of others and it naturally drove his business.

Knowing Who You Are and Defining Your Unique Selling Proposition

After my first month of getting oriented with the team and understanding how I fit in, Ryan and I began to spend a lot of time defining our team and our value proposition. This culminated in the preparation of a client presentation which included a very strong "sales pitch" for our team and a marketing plan that we felt answered every question a Buyer or Seller could have regarding what we do for them.

What Sets You Apart?

It was a cool early Spring morning and the robins had just arrived back from their winter vacation, signalling a turn in the weather and an inevitable turn in the real estate market. I had arrived early to start the coffee and prepare for my scheduled meeting with Ryan. While I hoped to have an hour or so to myself to gather my thoughts, Ryan came through the door moments after the last drips of coffee fell from the filter and into the glass pot.

"Good morning Alan!" he said coming through the door with his old soft leather briefcase in hand. "I didn't expect to see you here, and I certainly didn't expect coffee. What a treat."

"Good morning Ryan," I said, faking a smile and a little disappointed by the interruption. "I didn't expect you either."

"I expect you must have come in early for a reason, so I'll leave you to your work so you'll be ready for our meeting at 9:00."

"Thanks Ryan. I didn't get a chance to answer the email you sent me yesterday, but I know you wanted me to respond to it before our meeting." I appreciated his courtesy.

He laughed, "Ha! Like two peas in a pod! I'm here to do the same thing!"

Ryan 's email wasn't long, but it had some thought provoking questions in it. I looked back on it to be sure I was on the right track before putting pen to paper:

Good afternoon Alan,

Thank you for agreeing to meet with me tomorrow morning to discuss how we are going to position our team and develop a strategy for communicating our message to our potential clients. One of the greatest and most helpful things I ever did when starting out in this business was to develop my marketing message to my clients, and while it wasn't perfect, and it changed over time, it was something that helped me always stay focused:

"MARKETING YOUR HOME FOR ALL IT'S WORTH!"

Now that we're working together, I believe we need to review and modify that message to ensure our marketing message aligns the benefits of working with our team with the needs of our clients.

In marketing terms, the experts refer to this 'description' as a Unique Selling Proposition (USP) and it is something that needs to roll off our tongues whenever we describe what it is we offer our clients. There are four major steps to developing our USP.

1. Define our target market.

2. Define the problems we solve.

3. List the benefits we offer that our competitors don't.

4. Make a "pledge" to our clients that also serves to remind us of our commitments to ourselves and each other.

Once we've done this, we need to rework and massage all the information we compile into a paragraph that we can commit to, and then boil it down to a single sentence or phrase that will become our marketing message.

Because we work in such a small market, our "target markets" are pretty broadly defined, but in a nutshell: People who own property or want to purchase property within a 30 kilometre radius of our office.

While it would be great to specialize on a particular segment of that market, like the high end waterfront homes, I have analyzed the sales data and there simply isn't sufficient opportunity in any particular market segment to provide for our needs.

I thought we could meet tomorrow and spend whatever time it takes to do the other 3 steps. Before we meet I want us both to compile a list of descriptive words of that describe our own attributes and characteristics as well as a list that describes each other's. This will help us immensely when developing the list of benefits we offer our clients.

See you tomorrow!

Ryan

Confident that I understood what he was after, I started in on my first page, which I titled "Descriptive Words About Ryan"

1. Wise

2. Experienced

3. Knowledgeable

4. Practical

5. Professional

6. Warm Hearted

7. Good spirited

8. Assertive

9. Connected

10. Respected

11. Wealthy

12. Resourceful

13. Courageous

14. Successful

15. Creative

16. Thoughtful

17. Strong negotiator

18. Educated

19. Involved

20. Generous

21. Protective

With longer and longer pauses coming between descriptive, I decided to turn the page on my yellow lined pad and started in on a new list titled, surprisingly, "Descriptive Words About Alan."

1. Youthful

2. Energetic

3. Tech Savvy

4. Enthusiastic

5. Confident

6. Ethical

7. Trained

8. Professional

9. Driven

10. Entrepreneurial

11. Personable

12. Community minded

13. Helpful

14. Determined

15. Creative

16. Artistic

17. Honest

I felt like I was scraping the bottom of the barrel. I thought to myself, *"If I were in the market for a Realtor® why would I chose myself?"* and the immediate answer to the question scared me... *"I wouldn't."*

I was reminded about how fortunate I was to have aligned myself with an experienced Realtor® and it made me further appreciate the idea of apprenticeships of all kinds. I would never hire an inexperienced carpenter to build my house, but I would certainly hire one to work under the tutelage of a trusted contractor... So how was I going to find the confidence to sell myself to potential clients looking to sell their house? For the time being, I would lean on Ryan to help me.

18. Resourceful…

19. Committed to excellence

20. Networked

21. Team player

22. Hungry to learn

23. Motivated.

I put my head in my hands and scratched my scalp with my fingertips… hoping for more inspiration.

"How are you making out over there?" I asked Ryan, who was leaning back in his chair, obviously searching for his own words.

"I think I'm out of ideas," he said. "Are you ready to share notes?"

"Sure."

I moved over to the empty seat across from him and lay my yellow pad on the table, then slid it across to him. He did the same with his binder.

"Quality over quantity I see," I said with a grin. Ryan's list for himself was short:

Educated, professional, sincere, strong willed, forward thinking, future focused, experienced, knowledgeable, caring, empathetic.

I put a tick above the ones that stood out to me. "For me, what sets you apart from other Realtors® is your professionalism and commitment to your clients. I've never seen someone go to bat for their clients like you do."

"Thanks Alan," he replied. "I'm actually kind of moved by your list. I was expecting 'hot headed' and 'stubborn' to be there."

"I knew I forgot something!" I laughed. "Anything ring true to you?"

"Well, I'd say the strongest common thread relates to my experience and professionalism along with my commitment to my clients."

"I agree. And I think those are all attributes I would look for in a Realtor®."

"Me too," he said, nodding his head while reviewing the things I had written about myself.

I returned to his binder and looked down the list at his thoughts about me.

Honest, straight forward, hardworking, comfortable with technology, creative, helpful, funny, diligent, passionate, intelligent.

I put a tick over "straight forward" and "helpful," both or which struck a chord.

"Hmmm..." said Ryan, tapping his pencil on his lower lip. "Very good."

"Anything stand out?"

"I'm looking for reasons that I'd hire you to sell my house, and I'd say it's something that neither of us put on our list."

"Oh ya?" I asked, expecting a joke out of him.

"Yes," he said, putting the notepad down and looking me in the eye. "You have a reputation of being trustworthy. In my opinion, that is priceless."

I appreciated the sentiment, and on reflecting for a second, I nodded my head in agreement. "I guess so," I said.

"In my mind, it trumps everything else. Your trustworthiness along with your enthusiasm and technical proficiency would all be reasons I would hire you."

"You would hire me?" I asked, surprised by the idea.

"No… But I'd hire the team you work with," he replied with a wink.

I exchanged his binder for my notepad and we spent another few minutes scratching down other ideas, stroking out others, and trying to come up with a short list of two or three words which best described us.

"OK," I said eager to move on to the next part of developing our message. "We agree that what sets you apart is your PROFESSIONALISM, DEDICATION and EXPERIENCE and what sets me apart is my TRUSTWORTHINESS, ENTHUSIASM and TECHNICAL EXPERTISE."

"I like it," he replied. "That really helps us define what makes each of us special, which also helps us start to define what makes our team special."

I wrote the descriptives out on two yellow sheets in large letters with a felt pen, one for him and one for me, and put them up with a thumbtack on a cork board in the office with a real sense of accomplishment. Just then Kim walked through the door.

"Good morning Gentlemen," she said suspiciously, surprised to see us obviously so entrenched in something so early in the morning. "What are you two up to?"

"Hi Kim," Ryan replied. "Alan and I are working on developing a message for our marketing — a 'tagline' if you like — that will help us define why people should work with our team."

"That sounds interesting," she said, turning to look at the two sheets on the cork board. "I like your lists."

"Do you?" I asked sincerely. "These are the things that we think sum up why someone might hire each of us as their Realtors®. Would you agree?"

"PROFESSIONALISM, DEDICATION and EXPERIENCE... TRUSTWORTHINESS, ENTHUSIASM and TECHNICAL EXPERTISE," she read aloud. "That's good. But I don't think I'd hire you Alan because you are enthusiastic... I'd hire you because you're so helpful. Other than that I think it's great."

Kim headed to her desk and Ryan and I looked at each other with a smile.

"Helpful?" Ryan asked.

"Sure. Anyone can be enthusiastic, but it doesn't mean they could help me buy or sell a house," Kim said. "But I'd call Alan because I know he's happy to help."

"It's simple... but true!" said Ryan.

We talked it through for a while before we agreed to re-write the lists, making a couple of changes. The first page simply read: Ryan is caring, professional and experienced. The second page read: Alan is trustworthy, helpful and tech savvy.

"OK, now what about me?" asked Kim with a wink. "Am I a part of the team?"

Ryan looked a little embarrassed by not including Kim in the discussion from the start. "Of course you are Kim, and you are a big part of what differentiates us from our competition. Most Realtors® don't have assistants that keep everything on track and I stress how valuable that is to everyone I meet."

"I'm just teasing. You boys keep fluffing up your feathers and I'll make sure no one bothers you!"

Ryan and I laughed awkwardly, not exactly sure how Kim was feeling.

"Thanks Kim, I appreciate your help," Ryan said as he took his coffee cup and headed for a refill. "Do you want some more coffee Alan?"

"I'd love some thanks," I said, passing him my cup. "Hey Ryan I think we should have put "helpful" on your list too!" I said, recognizing that the adjective really was a simple but important part of why people made their hiring decisions. "At the end of the day, helping people is really what we do!"

The Services We Provide

Ryan turned back a few pages in his binder, looking at a list he had written a few days before. "The next thing for us to do is to consider the problems we solve for our clients."

"No problem," I said, smiling.

"Let's just review the process of buying a home and all the things that we do for our clients, then we'll move on to selling a home. Alan, can you write this stuff down?"

"Sure thing." I started taking notes as he spoke, adding items of my own as we went along.

BUYERS:

1. Explain agency and responsibilities under applicable statutes and laws.

2. Consult with and provide information on neighbourhoods, schools and market conditions

3.   Consider financing requirements and associated costs

4.   Make introductions and recommendations on mortgage brokers financial institutions

5.   Source suitable properties and provide insights and recommendations

6.   Arrange viewings

7.   Conduct viewings

8.   Prepare legally binding offers with appropriate terms, based on clients' needs

9.   Make recommendations on offer price and terms

10.   Negotiate offers

11.   Notify all parties of successful conclusion to negotiations, or repeat from step 6

12.   Recommend and introduce building inspectors, contractors, lawyers and notaries

13.   Provide assistance and access for inspections

14.   Secure and review title searches and Property Condition Disclosure Statements

15.   Secure and review strata minutes, bylaws and rules if necessary

16.   Review reports and inspections

17.   Renegotiate offer if necessary. If unable to renegotiate, repeat from step 6

18.   Remove subjects if satisfied

19.   Provide copies of contracts, inspections and title are provided to lenders if required

20.   Secure deposit and deposit into trust account as per the Real Estate Services Act

21.   Prepare transaction record sheet

22.   Ensure information on the transaction is conveyed to buyer's and seller's lawyers

23.   Monitor closing proceedings and assist clients and lawyers if required

24.   Ensure insurance is secured and utilities are transferred by buyers

25.   Ensure keys are secured from Selling Agent on possession day and deliver to buyer

26.   Conduct walk through inspection with client to ensure all is in order

27.   Liaise with Seller's agent if there are unresolved issues

28.   Provide thoughtful closing gift

29.   Follow up with the buyer to ensure they are satisfied

"Is that it?" I asked. "And people say we charge too much!"

Ryan smiled. "The reality is, we often go through nearly the entire process and never get a deal to closing... which means we don't get paid at all, but that's the nature of our business. OK - you start the list for the Sellers."

"All right," I said getting my pen back to the paper and calling things out as I wrote them down.

SELLERS:

1.   Review the Working with a Realtor® Brochure to explain agency relationship and what should be expected from a Realtor®

2.   Secure information on the subject property from local government, paid online sources and privileged information via the MLS (Multiple Listing Service)

3.   Order and pay for title search to ensure ownership rights and other charges which could affect value

4.   Visit property and attempt to determine property boundaries, service connections, and any other relevant features on title

5.   Inspect and measure buildings and improvements and conduct preliminary inspect for obvious deficiencies, within reason

6.   Provide recommendations on decorating, staging and repairs

7.   Recommend contractors, stagers, and other professionals

8.   Source information on comparable sales, listings and expired listings

9.   Analyze comparable properties and develop recommended asking price

10.   Provide a comprehensive argument with suggested market value and recommended list price based on information gathered

11.   Develop and provide a property specific marketing plan

12. If selected, prepare listing agreement with schedule of services

13. Negotiate listing price and duration of listing agreement

14. Complete MLS Data Information Form

15. Review Contract of Purchase and Sale document to prepare sellers when offers are received

16. Identify client for Federal Government by verifying appropriate identification and completing Individual Identification Record

17. In the event the owner is a corporation, secure and review incorporation documents and record Corporate Identification Record

18. In the event that the owner is a non-resident, review appropriate information and discuss withholding tax ramifications. Recommend appropriate lawyers / accountants

19. Review Capital Gains Tax implications

20. Review GST / PPT and other tax burdens

21. Review closing costs

22. Hire and pay for appropriate professionals including photographers, virtual tour companies, ad copywriters and graphic artists for feature sheet, brochure and website

23. Submit appropriate paperwork to the Brokerage and upload to MLS

24. Review marketing material with client and amend as necessary

25. Hire sign production and installation company

26.   Prepare comprehensive electronic information package for distribution to interested parties

27.   Conduct Realtor® "Whisper Campaign" to build awareness and create demand

28.   Advertise and conduct open house tours

29.   Respond to inquiries from the public and other Realtors®

30.   Be present at showings if requested

31.   Present and review all offers with sellers

32.   Negotiate favourable terms

33.   Continue to advertise and market the property until unconditional offer is secured

34.   Recommend lawyers and notaries for closing

35.   Convey documents and instructions to lawyers and notaries

36.   Provide keys to buyers or buyers' agents

37.   Assist in resolving any issues after closing

Ryan and I looked at each other, trying to think of anything else. "Sheesh!" I said. "That's something else! I hadn't really thought about all the things we bring to the table."

"Isn't it though?" said Ryan. "It's a good reminder to me as to why we never cut our commissions."

"So, based on these lists, I'd say we solve all kinds of problems for our clients. I don't think that the average person could do it without us," I said. "Connecting people to trusted professionals, providing information that they don't have ready access to, negotiating, getting them in to see properties, helping them value their homes, dealing with problems that arise, marketing and advertising, covering lots of costs up front... like I say, what we do is HELP people."

"That's not very sexy though," said Ryan. "Is it?"

"Uh... No," said Kim, apparently not as interested in her spreadsheet as we thought. "How about 'Provide Assistance'?"

"My brain hurts. Alan, why don't we take a 10-minute break and get some fresh air?" he said.

We headed outside and took the path to the dock. "Ryan, I know you said it isn't very sexy, but when it boils right down to it, helping people is really all we do," I said.

"And helping people is an honourable thing Alan. But does it adequately describe how we solve problems for our clients? If so, isn't 'helping people' too general? Doesn't everybody in a service industry 'help' their customers?"

"Sure. But I don't think the help that most service people provide has the same kind of value that the help we provide does," I replied, gaining some clarity through the conversation. "The hairdresser 'helps' you by making sure you look good, but in terms of value, the potential cost of a bad haircut is limited."

"Not if you ask my wife!" he shot back.

"OK, but you see my point," I replied. "If we screw up, the costs can be life changing. If we do a good job, the value is undeniable. The help we offer is so valuable, because without us our clients stand to make monumental errors that could really affect their family's future."

Ryan looked out over the water and then returned his gaze to me. "You're starting to build a pretty compelling case Mr. Stewart.

Maybe a sexy selling point shouldn't be part of my objective here. Maybe I'm thinking too far ahead."

"Hey, I'm no expert in this stuff, I just think that helping people is at the core of what we do."

"I have to agree Alan."

We returned to the office where Kim was talking to someone on the phone. "We'll look forward to seeing you on Tuesday then. Thank you for the call," she said, hanging up the phone. "Ryan, I've booked you for a meeting with a nice young couple from Washington that would like to meet with you on Tuesday afternoon when they arrive to start their home search. They weren't exactly sure of when they will arrive, but they'll give us a call when they reach the ferry terminal in Vancouver."

"Thanks Kim," said Ryan. "I'm sure we'll be able to help them out."

As we were sitting back down to the table, the door opened again. "Good morning everyone!" said a distinguished looking gentleman with grey hair and an engaging smile. "How are we doing?"

Ryan quickly rose up and made a move towards him, obviously pleased to see him. "John Duma! Good to see you, old man. It's been too long."

The two shook hands vigorously before Mr. Duma broke it off and made his way over to Kim who had stood to meet him. "This is the lady I really came to see!" he said, giving Kim a big hug that Kim seemed truly happy to return.

"Hi John. How great to see you," Kim said. "Is Marion with you?"

"No Kim, she's not. She had to stay in town as her hip has been really bothering her."

"Oh what a shame," Kim said with a frown. "Please give her my regards. John, this is Alan Stewart, a new member of our team."

"Hello Alan!" he said enthusiastically, stretching out his hand. "How are you?"

"I'm great, thank you. It's nice to meet you."

Ryan took charge. "John, please have a seat. What do you take in your coffee?"

"Just black. Thanks."

John took off his coat and hung it on the back of the chair. He sat down beside me taking a look at the notes on the table. "So what are you guys up to? Looks like I interrupted something."

"Actually John," said Ryan, "you're exactly the guy to help us out. We're just reviewing some of our marketing material and we could really use some input on why our customers hire us."

"Well I guess I would know!" John let out a laugh that was a few decibels higher than what the occasion called for, but endearing just the same. "Alan, I've bought and sold more than a dozen homes from the old fart! But I'm not sure who's further ahead... me or Ryan?"

"I don't think it's even close John," retorted Ryan. "If it were me, I'd be driving your Porsche and you'd be driving my old Volvo."

"I know, I know..." said John looking at me. "Ryan's actually helped me make a lot of money in real estate Alan. But he's helped me lose a few bucks too!"

Ryan put John's coffee down in front of him. "John, I really do want to ask you some questions but was there a reason for your visit?"

"Not really. I was kind of bored without Marion around, so I just thought I'd check in. I like the price of the coffee in this establishment!"

"I'm glad you did," said Ryan. "But today you have to pay for your coffee."

"Then I guess I'll be on my way!" said John, smiling as he stood to grab his coat.

Ryan grabbed him by the shoulder and said, "Sit down, sit down. No cash required, just some input."

"Alright. But remember, you get what you pay for!" he laughed.

"John, you've been working with me for a long time now, and I'd really like to know why you keep coming back. It would really help us in putting together our marketing message if we could get some honest feedback from our clients."

"Why do I keep coming back? That's a damn good question. I guess because I'm a sucker for nice people and cheap coffee." John laughed, along with the rest of us. "No, no. I'm just kidding. I can tell you exactly why I keep coming back. Because I trust you. Because you've proven yourself time and again to be looking out for me and you haven't given me any reason to change."

Ryan and Kim looked humbled and blushed a little.

"Thank you John," said Ryan. "That means a lot."

"Well it's true. And I don't care what anybody else says about you Ryan." We all laughed again. "Remember when you wouldn't let me buy that place on the highway as an investment property because you didn't think the location was right for what we wanted to do? I was ready to write the cheque, of which you would have received a healthy percentage, and you refused to write the contract. That kind of integrity is rare my friend."

"So the fact that I wouldn't take your money made you want to work with me more?" said Ryan. "I'm not sure I want that to be part of our marketing message!"

"It wasn't the fact that you wouldn't take the money. It was the fact that you felt strongly enough about your professional opinion and that you cared enough about Marion and me not to get involved in what you thought was a bad deal."

"Which I still say it was!" injected Ryan. "Even though I know you still aren't convinced."

"We'll never know Ryan, but Marion and I earned a lot of respect for you that day regardless of whether or not it was the right decision," John said and then took a big gulp of his coffee.

Kim entered the conversation. "John, we're struggling with whether or not 'helping' or 'providing assistance' is sufficient to describe what we do. What do you think?"

"I think that's at the core of your business, but it isn't just helping or providing assistance that makes what you guys do special," he said putting down his coffee and putting his hand over his chest. "It's about the fact that you guys really give a damn about your customers. And that kind of help is hard to find."

"So it's about trust and caring?" I asked.

"It is Alan. I could pay a lawyer less money to put together an offer on properties I buy than Ryan gets paid, and let's face it Ryan, I bring you most of the deals we put together, but I know that Ryan is going to do three things for me that I wouldn't get from a lawyer behind a desk. First, he's going to help me with valuing the property, and that objective opinion has saved me a boat full of cash."

"Interesting," I said, taking notes. "Is that because he's not emotionally attached to the property?"

"Exactly. And he obviously knows the market better than someone like me who just parachutes into it from time to time. Secondly, he helps me in structuring an offer that protects me as a result of everything he knows about the area... risks that a lawyer behind a desk would never think of."

"Like what?" I asked naively.

"Like the time when I bought a property to subdivide that looked too good to be true," John said, looking at Ryan. "And this old boy saved my bacon because he had attended a Council meeting and knew that the municipality was planning on rezoning the entire area to larger parcels sizes because of the watershed. Without him I would have cut the cheque for the purchase price without blinking. Instead, we recalculated our offer based on what we were going to be able to do with the property and included a copy of the minutes from that meeting in our offer. Alan, it saved me almost a quarter of a million dollars."

"I'm starting to see why you like him!" I laughed. "But wouldn't you have done your own due diligence and found out about it?"

"Maybe... but that's a whopper of a maybe. All I know is that Ryan and Kim have my back and I trust them, and that's good enough for me," John said smiling at Ryan and Kim both. "And finally, I've seen him at work negotiating and I believe that his industry knowledge is what enables him to be so effective. You simply can't effectively negotiate without a thorough understanding of all the issues."

"So if someone asked you to describe why you use Ryan's team to help you with buying and selling properties, how would you sum it up in one sentence?" I asked John.

"I use them because…." he paused and took a moment to finish off his coffee, "because they are caring, competent professionals that understand my goals and help me in achieving them. That's it."

"That's good enough for me," said Ryan as he sat back in his chair and put his hands behind his head like a high school student finishing a big assignment. "I love it."

Ryan stood, walked to the flip chart, and turned to a new page on which he wrote in a thick green marker:

> *"We are a team of caring real estate professionals who help our customers turn their dreams into reality by providing invaluable advice, proven marketing strategies and expert negotiating skills."*

"John, your cup of coffee was the best investment I've ever made!" Ryan said as he shook John's hand. "You've helped us define our Unique Selling Proposition."

"I'm glad to be able to have helped out, Ryan," John replied. "It's nice to be able to return a favour."

With that, John put his coffee cup on the counter, said his goodbyes and gave Kim a big hug before heading for the door. The room seemed a lot emptier after he left and I remember feeling a little sad that he had gone.

Defining Ourselves

It felt like we had just finished a marathon together. There was an energy in the air and Ryan shook both Kim's hand and mine in a gesture of appreciation. When Ryan wrote our new Unique Selling Proposition on the flip chart, I felt a tingle run through my body that reminded me of when I used to touch a 9 volt battery to the tip of my tongue. It was electric, and I would come to recognize it later in life as an "alignment." It was my body and soul telling me that everything was in order. I first understood what it meant at the Chiropractor's office, when I experienced the same rush of energy when my spine was correctly aligned through a disturbing crunch inflicted on me by the Doctor.

Ryan, Kim and I had done a little bit of chiropractic work on our business by taking a good hard look at what made us special, and it left us all energized and aligned. We knew exactly what we had to do to succeed: become experts in our craft and focus on our customers' needs.

"Thank you both so much. I'm really, really happy with what we were able to accomplish today in such a short time," said Ryan as he looked us each in the eyes. "And John's reminded me of something else. He's reminded me about the importance of not only our client's dreams, but our dreams as well."

"You are welcome Ryan," replied Kim. "It's people like John that make it worth coming to work in the morning. I love that guy!"

CHAPTER 2

THE REALTOR REFERRAL GARDEN

Outside of Ryan 's office was a very productive apple tree that produced plenty of product for Sue's delicious pies. In the fall, Ryan asked me if I wouldn't mind helping him pick the apples with him and I was happy to oblige.

"I'll tell you what Ryan," I said with a wink. "I'll pick that tree clean with you if you can promise me one of Sue's pies!"

"That's a deal. Why don't you bring the girls with you too? It'll be fun."

So on a bright and sunny Saturday afternoon I arrived at work with my wife Paola and our three daughters, Mackenzie, Samantha and Hannah, ready to reap the year's harvest.

"Hello everyone!" Sue said, coming out of the office with a large brimmed straw hat and carrying baskets for each of the girls. "Are you ladies going to help your Dad pick our apples?"

Four year old Samantha buried her face into my thigh and held on, embarrassed for some reason by the question. Mackenzie, who was six, was too excited to hold back and ran towards Sue, knowing that she often had treats for them.

"Yes we are!" she shrieked. "Are those baskets for us?"

"How did you know?" Sue replied as she separated the baskets and asked Mackenzie to pass one to Samantha and me.

"Mackenzie has been charged up about this since I told her about it on Tuesday," I said. "Especially when I told her we might get a pie out of the deal."

We all laughed and Mackenzie lit up like a lightbulb when Sue promised her and the girls a little pie all of their own.

The girls weren't much help, but enjoyed running around the yard while I fetched the ladder from around the side of the house. When I returned, Ryan had also made his way out of the office and looked far more casual than usual in a pair of jeans and a plaid flannel shirt.

"Oh thanks Alan. We'll need that ladder in a little while, but let's start with the low hanging fruit."

"It's your tree," I said, "and I'm no expert in apple picking so I'll follow your lead."

Ryan and I started on opposite sides of the tree, carefully twisting and picking the ripe apples and exciting the girls when one would accidentally fall from a branch as a result of our moving the branches. Sue and my wife sat together in the sun with baby Hannah being bounced gently on Sue's lap.

"Girls, come here for a second," Ryan said to the older two who came over, panting from their skipping around the yard. "Can I share a lesson with you that my Dad shared with me a long time ago?"

"Sure," said Mackenzie.

"Soor," echoed Samantha, as well as she could.

Ryan squatted down next to them and picked up one of the apples that had fallen to the ground. "My Dad told me that the secret to success is to always pay the most attention to the lowest hanging fruit. Do you know why?" He passed the apple to Mackenzie who looked it over.

"No. Why?" she asked.

"Because far too many people miss the opportunities that are right in front of them. Instead they focus on the fruit that's out of reach."

"Do you mean like me heading for the ladder before we had picked all these apples right in front of us?" I asked.

"Exactly," said Ryan, never taking his eyes off of Mackenzie. "You see, Mackenzie and Samantha, sometimes we think that the apples way up there at the top of the tree must taste better than these ones down here because they are harder to get to. But in reality, these apples down here are just as delicious and much easier to get."

"But they are still too high for me to reach," Mackenzie said, crossing her arms and putting out her bottom lip.

"Well we can fix that," Ryan said, standing up and grabbing his step stool. "Here, let me hold your hand and you can use this."

While Mackenzie made her way up the step stool, Ryan continued, "And the worst part is that sometimes when you go to all that work to try and get the apples way up at the top of the tree, you wind up damaging the fruit at the bottom... and that is a real shame."

I walked towards them and picked up Samantha to lift her up to the lowest branches. "Go ahead Sammy. Can you pick an apple?" I asked.

The girls each took their prizes and ran over to show their Mom.

"Look Mommy!" cried Mackenzie. "Ryan helped me pick an apple. Can I eat it?"

"Of course you can," said Sue. "There are plenty more for the pies."

Ryan and I continued to work and I asked him about the lesson he shared with the girls. "So what kind of low hanging fruit are we missing in our business, Ryan?"

"Referrals," he said, barely missing a beat.

"Sounds like you've been thinking about that!" I laughed.

"Absolutely. It's been a long time since I had thought about that saying of my Dad's," Ryan said, continuing to pull fruit from the branches. "It's been years since I really focused on that end of the business, and it's a real shame."

I scratched my chin with the back of my hand as I spoke, "But I thought we did a pretty good job of trying to get referrals from our clients Ryan? I mean we always add, 'The highest compliment we can be paid is when you send us a referral!' to our newsletters and ads, and we send out an awful lot of thank you notes and gift cards to people who send us those referrals. What more can we do?"

"While there's lots of room for improvement with our client referrals, I think we're missing the low hanging fruit. What group of people do you know that actually look for referrals as part of their everyday working lives?"

"You mean the way that Realtors® do?" I asked.

"I mean exactly the way Realtors® do!" he paused, struggling to pull another apple from the tree until it snapped off the branch. "When I first started in the business in Victoria in 1991, I spent about half of my time building a referral network with other Realtors® and influential people, and it made all the difference."

Identifying Your Referral Garden

According to Ryan, he had created what he referred to as a 'referral garden' in various communities. His system was simple but brilliant, and according to Ryan, incredibly effective.

"If you want to build a great Realtor referral network, you have to nurture it the same way you have to nurture a garden," said Ryan. "You have to plant the right seeds, provide the right water and food, and make sure to keep the weeds in check."

"Okay, I'll bite," I said, accidentally breaking a branch while pulling too hard on an apple that wasn't quite ready to let go. "Tell me about the seeds, the food and water and the weeds."

"Well, planting the right seeds meant taking the time to find the right people in the right areas to add to my referral network. Early on in my career I would always ask the conveyance department or the listing agent where the buyers on a property had moved from," Ryan laughed. "It actually started to drive people crazy. While everyone else wanted to know how much a property sold for, I just wanted to know where the buyers were from."

"Clever," I said, nodding. "So that helped you to figure out where you should be looking for Realtor referrals?"

"Yes, but also where I needed to start making relationships with office staff and managers."

"Why office staff and managers?" I asked, surprised that they would spin off many referrals.

Ryan raised his eyebrows when he looked at me and grinned. "Because Realtors® who don't know an agent in an area often reach out to their managers or receptionists for advice. And whenever anyone asked either of them for the name of an agent in Victoria, I wanted to be at the top of the list."

"How did you figure that out?" I wondered.

"Easy. Within my first two weeks on the job I needed a referral agent for my sister in Ontario and so I went straight to the Office Manager for help… and that got me thinking. If I was talking to my Manager for a referral, how many others were doing the same?"

"So you figured out that the Realtors®, staff and managers working in markets that had buyers moving to your market were low hanging fruit. They were in the garden in which you needed to plant seeds. Have I got that part of the analogy right?"

"Exactly," said Ryan, looking satisfied. "If I was going to invest in this garden, I wanted to get the best return on investment I could."

"So how did you invest in them?" I asked. "Was it some sort of kickback?"

Ryan held the apple in his hand out in front of him and between us. "Alan, if you want a tree to produce fruit, do you only give it water and add fertilizer to the soil after it's produced a crop? Or do you give the tree what it needs knowing that if you do it will give you what you want?" Ryan tossed the apple over to me and I looked at it.

"You give it what it needs until it gives you what you need," I said, tossing it back to him. "So what do managers and staff need to help them produce referrals?"

Ryan bit into the apple and wiped the juice from his beard with his forearm. As he finished chewing he said, "Just a little love and attention Alan. We humans are interesting creatures and I was just starting to appreciate the power of reciprocation."

Ryan went on to tell me all about his strategy, which seemed slightly contrived but which I knew would be effective.

A student of human nature, Ryan understood two things very well. First, that in order to be thought OF, you need to be thoughtFUL; and second, that the law of reciprocity meant that people feel obliged to return favours or acts of kindness. Ryan's referral program was founded on these two simple concepts which he had printed on a poster in his office:

To be remembered:

1. Be thoughtful about other people's needs

2. Take action every day to satisfy those needs

Any gardener will tell you that to keep a garden alive, you have to provide water. To make a garden thrive, you have to add the right nutrients and fertilizer. Ryan had realized that to make his business thrive, he was going to have to add something to nourish his relationships and make him stand out. He asked himself a simple question: Who in my life would I refer someone to, and why? His loyalty to a particular mortgage broker provided the answer.

Thoughtfulness in Action

According to Ryan, nobody exemplified thoughtfulness better than Sarah River who seemed to have an endless amount of time and energy to focus on the Realtors® working from Ryan 's office. Ryan joked with his Manager one day about how hard it must be for Sarah to prospect for new business when she spent all her time having lunch and coffee with Realtors®.

"Are you kidding?" the Manager said. "She IS prospecting!"

It hit Ryan like a ton of bricks. Sarah wasn't being insincere or manipulative in taking care of Realtors®, she was nurturing relationships with the people who were most likely to refer her business. Brilliant.

On arriving at work one day Ryan was pleasantly surprised to find a neatly wrapped gift on his desk with a little card attached that simply said, "Ryan." He unwrapped the gift, which he knew instinctively was a hardcover book, and was delighted to find a copy of Jack Canfield's "The Success Principles" inside. He opened the cover and read the handwritten note. "Dear Ryan. I saw this book and it made me think of you. Here's to YOUR success. Sarah."

Ryan and Sarah had been talking the two weeks before about some of his frustrations around his productivity and how he had such high aspirations for himself. The fact that someone cared enough to listen, had him on their mind for a couple of weeks, spent earnest money on a gift and then took the time to deliver it in a special way made Ryan warm all over.

"Sarah," Ryan said when he heard her pick up on the other end of the line. "This is Ryan and I just got your wonderful gift. I can't tell you how much I appreciate it!"

"Hi Ryan," Sarah replied with a smile in her voice. "I'm so glad you like it! I don't know if you remember me talking about the book when we had coffee a couple of weeks ago, but it's really one of the most powerful things I've ever read. When I saw it I couldn't resist."

"Well you've really made my day and I just wanted you to know that. I can't remember anyone doing something like this for me."

"And that makes my day Ryan. I hope you like it."

"I'm sure I will Sarah. Thanks again and we'll catch up soon."

Hanging up the phone and looking at the book, Ryan felt good and he was proud of the fact that he made the call to Sarah because she felt great about the 'transaction' as well.

A month later Ryan picked up *The Success Principles* and opened it to Chapter 15. He had been methodically making his way through the book, making notes in the columns, and trying to implement as many of the strategies as he could. He thought of Sarah and how powerful this gift had been and he thought about how he could return the favour. Then he realized that over the past month he had referred three people to Sarah for mortgage advice. When was the last time someone had referred three people to him for real estate advice in a month? What a powerful, tangible lesson on the power of investing in relationships in some way.

That was the day that Ryan set out a plan to plant, water and fertilize his referral garden.

Planning Out the Garden

Ryan's objective was to be the first Realtor that came to mind when influential people in complementary markets thought about real estate in Victoria, just the same way that Sarah River came to mind for him when he thought about mortgages. Through his research Ryan had plotted out where people had moved from by pushing white push pins into a map he had put on a cork board.

Understanding that consumers typically expected to be referred to Realtors® working under the same brand, Ryan decided to focus on his efforts on Royal LePage offices whenever possible and he put red push pins in the board to mark their locations.

While at first there didn't appear to be any patterns, it wasn't long before clusters started to form in certain towns and Ryan smiled every time he would add white pins to areas that had red pins. These red and white clusters told him exactly where he needed to be focusing his attention. He grouped them into three different categories.

The first group, and the largest by far, were the areas he could drive to within 2 hours but outside of his immediate selling area. In order to define how far away from Victoria Ryan would begin to stake out his trap line, he simply asked himself how far away he would be prepared to work with a Buyer. Ryan drew a black line around the boundary of the area he would consider working with clients and made a decision to focus his referral energy outside of this area.

While there were a lot of buyers coming to Victoria from within this region, Ryan felt his odds of earning referrals from offices in his immediate area were minimal. As a relatively hungry new Realtor®, he knew his boundaries were likely a little further out than many experienced agents but he didn't want to spend his energy on offices that would likely employ Realtors® like him that would be happy to sell in Victoria. Any referrals from these managers and staff would go to their own people.

That left him with 3 offices to really focus his attention on in his first group.

The second group were offices that were going to require a day trip to attend to, but which he could visit and get home to sleep in his own bed. Ryan knew that if he wanted to allow anytime to actually nurture relationships he would have to limit day trips to specific areas around the Lower Mainland of Vancouver and that it only made sense to focus his efforts on those areas with the greatest number of pins on the board, even though there may only be two or three, compared to the clusters on Vancouver Island.

The third group were offices that were going to require an overnight stay to travel to and take care of. There were only a few spots on the map that showed signs of promise, like Kelowna, Calgary and Edmonton.

Ryan 's plan was simple. Take the information he had compiled from his research, make a list of the Royal LePage offices in those communities, and make a list of the managers and the office reception staff. This list would form the basis of his garden and Ryan would treat it like any good salesperson's "A" list; he would water and nurture it with an expectation that it would bear fruit. But unlike the rest of the clients in Ryan 's database, which he only expected to participate in transactions every 4-6 years, Ryan expected the people on this list to provide him with a steady stream of referral leads.

Knowing that the Managers in the offices closest to home may well have existing connections in the Victoria market, Ryan recognized that he may have to nurture these relationships for some time before they started to deliver referrals, but he knew it was important to be the person that came to mind first and foremost. He remembered being told that to remain top of mind, a potential client or referral agents needed to see or hear from you 10 - 12 times a year, but the idea of being annoying and pushy made Ryan think of reasons why someone may want to hear from him that often.

"I want people to remember me, but not dread seeing me," Ryan said to his wife at the kitchen table one night. "I can't even remember the last time I heard from a salesperson in my life, but I can't imagine wanting to hear from someone every month!"

Sue looked up from her plate. "Dear, if you're going to be stopping by to see these people every month, you better show up with something."

Ryan remembered the gift of the book he had received from Sarah and how great it made him feel. "You've hit the nail on the head!" Ryan said excitedly. "Who doesn't like to see the delivery man show up with a gift?"

Planting the Seeds

Ryan thought about what he could do that would help him stand out in the minds of the Manager and his staff so that whenever a Realtor® would ask for a connection in Victoria, there is no way they wouldn't think of Ryan. He needed something that would be well received and help tie their memories to real estate in Victoria and him. There was a fantastic and very well known chocolate company in Victoria and Ryan knew exactly how he would start to build relationships with the people he needed to remember him. The next day Ryan drove to and asked to speak with the manager. A nice looking young lady with a slightly round face came out from the back.

"Hello. Can I help you?" she asked.

"I hope so," said Ryan. "I'm hoping you could help me in preparing a customized promotional item that I can use as a gift to build up my referral business?"

"What did you have in mind?" she asked.

Ryan went on to explain his idea. "I'm hoping that you could make a custom mold for me on the condition that I was willing to commit to a regular monthly order? And then we could make different types of chocolates that I could deliver as special gifts?"

"What a wonderful idea!" the gal behind the desk said. "What kind of budget do you have?"

"To be honest, I'm just starting out in my career, and I'm trying not to break the bank," said Ryan, a little ashamed. "But I do want to make sure that I make this worth your while and that's why I'd be prepared to give you a minimum order commitment for the first 6 months if you can offer me a bulk order price that I can get from you over time."

"To be honest, that works really well for us," she said, appreciating Ryan's desire to get the most from his budget. "We don't have the capacity to do this kind of stuff in one fell swoop, so if we can block it into our production schedules and have a minimum commitment, I think we can make it work."

Ryan smiled. "That's fantastic. Can I tell you what I had in mind?"

Ryan pulled a slip of paper from his pocket with some sketches on it and went on to explain the design he had thought of which encapsulated some of the most recognizable landmarks of Victoria, wildlife and a smiling image of Ryan behind a "For Sale" sign.

"Whoa! That's a lot of stuff to fit on a chocolate!" interrupted the Chocolatier. "Can I make a suggestion?"

Ryan was a little taken aback, but agreed that it might be too busy and asked for her help.

"From what you've told me, all you are trying to do is have people connect Victoria Real Estate with you. We already have a mold with the parliament buildings and Victoria written underneath. I think that would do it if it came from you… and we wouldn't have to charge you anything for the mold. It comes in a cellophane wrapper and you could easily put a sticker on it with your name and phone number."

"You know what," Ryan said, scratching his chin and looking at the sample she brought out from behind the counter, "it's perfect. Sometimes I overthink things, but you're absolutely right that it's the connection with Victoria that's important, and the fact that it is a gift coming from me forms the connection I'm looking for. Brilliant."

Ryan and the young gal spent some time reviewing the number of chocolates Ryan was going to need and based on Ryan's commitment to a minimum quantity, he was able to secure the chocolates at a wholesale price, plus a 15% up-charge for the store producing and applying the customer foil stickers which mimicked the store's own labels but had Ryan's information on them along with the store's.

"This is going to be a great trademark for you Ryan," said the clerk, shaking his hand as he left the store with a dozen samples of his new calling card in hand.

"I can't thank you enough," replied Ryan. "I think these are going to be really well received and I'm sure they will have people remembering me.

Ryan drove home, sampling one of his new chocolate bars and relishing the fact that it was a very high quality product and that he had negotiated a really fair price. The chocolate bars retailed for $3.49 a piece and given the store's reputation, the recipients would know that this wasn't a "cheap" gift. Ryan would be paying $2.00 each which he felt was money well spent. Time would tell.

Preparing the Feeding Schedule

Ryan now had to develop a plan of who to visit and how often. Just like any garden, he knew that he would have to pay a lot of attention to it in the beginning, but then his job would become easier. He needed a plan to be sure that he wouldn't drop the ball in the beginning. Over a cup of coffee at a local coffee shop overlooking Victoria's inner harbour, Ryan started putting a plan to paper.

A LIST OFFICES:

After careful consideration, Ryan broke his list of offices to service into three categories. His A List offices would be in those areas located within one day's drive of Victoria and on Vancouver Island. These were offices in which someone might have clients that are searching in "complementary areas" that those agents didn't service. Not only would these offices prove to be the easiest to build relationships with because of geography, but they were also the most likely sources of outgoing referral business. In other words, Ryan was more likely to refer business to those offices as he was to receive referrals from them.

There were 5 offices on Vancouver Island that fit the bill and which would be a top priority for Ryan. He would nurture these offices and ensure that they bore fruit.

B List Offices:

After paying attention to the home sales in his office, Ryan concluded that more people moved close to home than a long way away. Ryan returned to the map on his office wall with the red pins showing offices and the white pins showing where people were coming from and he quickly deduced that anyone within the Lower Mainland of Vancouver would be his B list offices. There were 10 offices in Vancouver and the surrounding area that Ryan added to his list.

From a cost standpoint, Ryan wanted to make sure that the Managing Broker and either the office manager or the front desk staff received one chocolate bar a month. Pretty simple math for his A and B list office referrals. He was going to need 2 chocolate bars at $2.00 each for 15 offices every month, which would mean a total budget of... $60 a month. Could that be right? Could he really touch some influential people in 15 different offices for less than $100? Done!

C List Offices:

Then Ryan considered his C List which would be targeted offices that were in areas of significant migration to Victoria but which he knew would be difficult to access personally. These would be long distance relationships. According to the data he was able to secure from the provincial government, the largest number of people moving to British Columbia came from Alberta and then Ontario. None of the other provinces even held a candle.

Ryan set his sights on Alberta and Ontario as his C List targets, and in particular Calgary, Edmonton, Ottawa and Toronto. While he knew that people would be moving to BC and to Victoria from other areas, he knew he couldn't manage to take care of everyone, so he chose to put his efforts into those areas with the most likelihood of success. Edmonton and Ottawa were both Capital cities, just like Victoria, and Toronto and Calgary were the most densified and richest markets of their kinds.

Calgary had 5 Royal LePage offices that Ryan thought warranted attention, Edmonton had 4, Toronto had 18 and Ottawa had 8. That was a total of 37 offices that would comprise Ryan 's C List. Ryan knew that he simply couldn't form the same kind of relationships with these offices that he would with the offices within his A List area, but that didn't mean he would develop a plan to ensure that at least the Managing Brokers in each of those offices would know him and associate him with Victoria Real Estate.

Watering Schedule

A LIST OFFICES

Ryan wanted to ensure that he developed a plan that would not be too onerous on him so as to make sure he could keep up with his duties. He knew that being top of mind meant that people should hear from him 10 - 12 times a year, or once a month to make it simple. While Ryan couldn't travel the country once a month, he knew that he could schedule a trip from his home to Campbell River, the most northern of the Vancouver Island A List offices, every 30 days.

Monday mornings were as good a time as any to find Managing Brokers in the office and so Ryan decided that on the second Monday of each month he would begin doing the rounds, leaving early and driving the 3 hours to Campbell River in order to arrive around 9:30am. The time alone was a welcome one for Ryan who loved listening to motivational tapes and audio books he borrowed from the library on the car stereo.

Ryan intended to build deep relationships with the brokers and staff in these A List offices, and so he allowed a total of 6 hours driving time and 30 minutes on average at each office, or a total of 8.5 hours. He expected that some office visits might be short in the beginning, but hoped he could extend his visits without being an intrusion over time. It was going to be a full day, and a full day away from his regular real estate practice, but Ryan knew it was the right thing to do in the long run.

B LIST OFFICES

The B List offices were a little more challenging, but Ryan knew that making the 2-hour ferry ride and building relationships with these people was important. While he couldn't commit to doing so monthly, he could manage to make a personal visit every other month. And Canada Post would take care of the months that he didn't make the trip. The cost of postage was a lot less than the price of the ferry ride!

Ryan decided that he would break the 10 offices up into two groups, which meant he would only make a personal visit to each office every 4 months. Ryan intended to combine the trip with personal visits to his friends and family in Vancouver, and when possible, overnight there as well whenever Sue could join him.

C LIST OFFICES:

The C List offices were too numerous and spread out to visit with any kind of regularity. These offices would be serviced differently and without the personal touch and relationship building that the A and B List offices would receive. He would "farm" these offices in the same way his Managing Broker had taught him to farm a geographical area around Victoria. But he knew he would need something more informative than a tasty treat arriving in the mail every month.

While he wouldn't be able to "press the flesh," Ryan decided that making introductory phone calls introducing himself and asking permission to send the C List Managing Brokers a tasty Victoria delight every month to help them remember him whenever they needed a referral agent in Victoria couldn't hurt in building rapport. He would also offer to act as a "complimentary service agent" whenever they, or one of their Realtors®, were in need of assistance in the Victoria area for witnessing documents, arranging facsimiles, or reviewing paperwork.

Ryan set to work on a spreadsheet onto which he would put each of the offices, sorted by areas, and which would include the names and contact information for each Managing Broker, which he could find online. He also left a field for the administrative staff, which he would start doing reconnaissance on as he made his rounds through the A and B List offices. This spreadsheet would also act as his mail-merge information for preparing the mailing labels he would need each month.

Nutrients and Sunlight

Lying in bed that night, too excited about this new program to sleep, Ryan felt his wife's hand take his. He was fortunate to have her and he couldn't help but feel grateful for Sue's suggestion of delivering gifts to the people he was going to be adding to his Realtor Referral Garden. Who didn't like receiving gifts?

"Honey, I am really pumped up about this Realtor Referral Garden idea," said Ryan quietly. "When Sarah River gave me that book, I felt really good. It was a dopamine rush, just knowing that someone cared enough to think of me and honour me with a gift and now I get to do the same for others."

Sue turned her head to look at him in the moonlight. "That's wonderful Ryan. I got a letter from my cousin Jane the other day and I felt the same way. It's nice to be thought of."

"Jane? You haven't heard from her in years. How is she?"

"She's seems to be doing alright. She had heard from my Aunt that you were selling real estate and so she sent a graph from her local paper in Oregon showing what's happening to housing prices there," replied Sue with a yawn. "I put it on your desk for you with a little yellow sticky note from her to you. She's cute."

Ryan gave his wife a kiss on the forehead and made a couple of notes in his bedside journal, not wanting to forget the idea that cousin Jane's letter had inspired. Ryan closed his eyes and smiled, knowing that he was onto something.

The next morning, with coffee in hand, Ryan made his way into his office and picked up the newspaper clipping from his desk. Just as he had expected, Jane had handwritten a little note for him on the yellow Post-it note. "Thinking of you and wishing you well! Jane." It added a personal touch to the newspaper that almost forced Ryan to read it out of respect for her efforts.

Ryan sat down, read the article and studied the graph, somewhat surprised by the fact that housing prices in Portland were continuing to decline, unlike what was happening in Victoria where things were steadily improving since a set back in the early 1980s.

The graph provided some quick insights into the Portland market in only a few seconds, and Ryan knew that adding a powerful, simple information piece would be an important part of building his reputation, in particular with his C List offices.

Ryan grabbed a lined notepad from his drawer and began to sketch out a very simple one-page marketing piece that he could easily update with market information and some useful information that would be appreciated and appropriate for the people in his Realtor Referral Garden. He envisioned it in black print on grey paper, set up to look like a mini newspaper front page. Working on a tight budget, Ryan didn't want to break the bank and reminded himself of how important it was to keep it simple enough to update in under an hour so as to ensure it got done.

He wrote a list of the things that needed to be incorporated into the one-page document, paying attention to think of the needs of the people who would be reading it, not his own.

Title: Victoria Update

1. Monthly Historical Median Price Graph provided by Victoria Real Estate Board

2. Sample listing showing what you get for your money in Victoria

3. Sales Meeting Ideas or Business Tip

4. Food or Drink Recipe

5. Joke or motivational quote

6. Ryan 's Contact Information with company logo

Simple but effective, so long as Ryan was diligent about getting it out the door on a regular basis. Turning on his computer, Ryan opened his word processing program and spent an hour preparing the template he would be happy with. Nothing too fancy, but he could quickly and easily populate it.

"What are you working on?" asked Sue who had come into the room unnoticed.

"Cousin Jane's newspaper article inspired me to create a little information piece that I'm going to deliver with the chocolate bars," he said, rocking back in his chair and allowing Sue to have a better look. "While it's going to be important to water and feed this garden, it also needs sunlight. I figured that to really make this garden come to life, we needed to provide some basic insights to the people we're trying to reach."

"But I thought you said you wanted to keep this simple so as to ensure that you didn't get too busy to get it done?" she reminded him.

"I wanted to create something easy to fill out so I'm sure to get it done. Our Real Estate Board sends us a graph every month that I'll put in the top section and everything else we can get online."

"That's something I could help you with, if you like?"

"Absolutely," said Ryan, grateful for the assistance. "I'm concerned that I'll drop the ball on this which might delay me getting these to the folks on my list. If you can commit to doing it every month it will keep me accountable to getting them done."

"You know I'm happy to help. I can even do the mailouts for you."

"Even better. That will just leave me with the sticky notes," Ryan said, leaning back into his desk and retrieving the yellow sticky note.

"Sticky notes?" Sue asked.

"Jane made this so much more personal and meaningful by just attaching a little handwritten note, so I thought I'd do the same for any of the ones that I can't hand deliver."

"I think this is going to be a lot of fun Ryan," Sue said, gently pushing Ryan aside and taking control of the computer. "I'm going to get started on finding a recipe and putting together our first edition!"

Ryan smiled, kissed Sue on the head, and headed to their bedroom to get ready for the day.

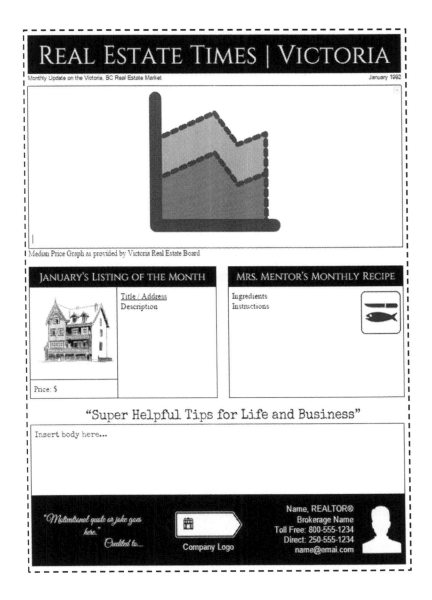

Getting Started

"Hello, may I please speak to Dave Schmidt?" Ryan said, slightly nervous about making his first appointment call to a Managing Broker in another office.

"One moment, please," returned the voice on the other end of the line.

Ryan scanned through his script one last time while the on-hold music played through his handset.

"This is Dave."

"Good morning Dave," Ryan started. "This is Ryan Campbell calling from Royal LePage in Victoria. How are you today?"

"I'm fine thanks Ryan," came the friendly reply which set Ryan's heart at ease. "How are things down South?"

"Things are fantastic here Dave. I'm new to Royal LePage and I wanted to reach out and introduce myself to you. I spoke with my Broker, Mike Peterson, and he said you were a good guy to know."

Dave laughed a little. "Mike Peterson said that!? Are you sure?"

Ryan joined Dave in the chuckle and he could tell it was going to be an easy call, given their mutual acquaintance with Ryan's broker.

"He sure did Dave, and I think he was being serious!" Another chuckle. "Listen Dave, I don't want to keep you but I'm heading up to Campbell River next Monday morning and I was hoping to drop by and drop off some really helpful information I've put together, along with a little treat from Victoria. Could I do that around 9:30 on Monday?"

"If you can make it a little earlier I'd appreciate it Ryan. We start our sales meeting at 9:30. If you want to stick around for that, I can introduce you to the rest of the gang in the office?"

Ryan could hardly believe it. "That would be great Dave. Can you tell me how many agents you have in your office? I'd like to bring a little treat for them too."

"We have a little over 30 Realtors®, but we only get about half of those out to our meetings," Dave said.

"I'm really looking forward to hearing more about what's happening in the Campbell River market and sharing a bit about what's happening down here with your Realtors®. I'll plan on being at your office at 9:00."

"Sounds good Ryan. Please pass my regards to Mike." There was a click at the other end and the line was disconnected. Ryan let out a sigh, reached his right hand over his left shoulder, and patted himself heartily on the back. "Fantastic!" he said out loud to himself. "If it's that easy to get in the door to a sales meeting, this program is going to be a huge success!"

It turned out that getting an audience with virtually every Managing Broker was nearly as easy, although being invited to attend sales meetings wasn't the norm. Because the offices all flew under the same franchise umbrella, there was an immediate camaraderie established whenever Ryan introduced himself.

Ryan continued calling all the offices on his A List, B list and finally on his C List until he had made a personal introduction to each of the Managing Brokers and had set tentative appointments to meet with them, agreeing that he would leave a little something for them in the event that they weren't there. Ryan was also able to secure the names of a dozen administrative staff that he wanted to be sure to take care of, and he did it all in one morning.

Now all that was left for Ryan to do was to ensure he had enough Newsletters, business cards and chocolate bars for the folks he would be meeting the following Monday, including 20 extra for anyone that attended the sales meeting in Campbell River. While Ryan was tempted to leave one for all the Realtors®, he was committed to nurturing relationships, and not prospecting to folks he had never met.

The Results

In Ryan's first month, having visited 5 offices on Vancouver Island and 5 offices in the Lower Mainland of Vancouver, Ryan received 2 referral leads and represented one of them in writing a contract on an executive home in James Bay. The net commission, after paying the 25% referral fee, was sufficient to fund the Realtor Referral Garden project for the next 2 years.

And the garden would continue to bear fruit for years to come. Not only did Ryan develop intimate friendships and begin to share ideas with many influential people in his industry on a regular basis, the referral agents that Ryan worked with were added to his Referral Garden list, which only caused it to grow. After his third full year in the business, 45% of all Ryan's new business was earned through the simple act of maintaining his relationships with the Managing Brokers, staff and loyal Realtors® he had come to know.

CHAPTER 3

OUTSIDE HELP

To help me realize my own dreams, Ryan had Kim make arrangements for me to attend an upcoming real estate seminar in Vancouver, led by an industry guru who was developing quite a following.

"Mr. Real Estate," as the guru liked to be called, wasn't a lot older than me, but the slicked back hair, red tie, crisp white shirt and pinstriped blue suit on his promotional photo reeked of success... and a little bit of arrogance. I knew nothing about the man but Ryan had attended a two-day seminar that he had hosted the previous year.

"Alan," Ryan said, "we're very fortunate to live and work in a place where the competition may not be as intense as it is in the big city. We don't have to break the bank on advertising to make our presence known because we can engage with nearly everyone in our community on a personal level. That's not the case in bigger cities. I want you to go to this seminar and see how we can take our business up a notch."

Having grown up in Vancouver, I was certainly aware of the benefits of working in a small town. It's much easier to connect with people in a small community because you wind up bumping into the same people whether you are working, volunteering, playing or just enjoying a meal at a local restaurant. It's much easier to hide when you're surrounded by hundreds of thousands of strangers... and it's also much harder to stand out.

I was excited about attending the event at the Hyatt Regency Hotel and had no problem rising at 5:00am to make the journey to the ferry and across to Vancouver. Because the ferries ran every two hours, the only way I could make it downtown in time was to catch the 6:30am ferry, putting me on the North Shore of Vancouver nearly 2 hours before I had to be there.

The night before I had ironed a white shirt and pressed a pair of slacks that I hadn't worn in nearly two years, only having needed them for weddings and funerals. I always liked dressing up a little as it gave me more confidence and made me feel a little powerful. I put on the clothes, pulled on a pair of tight black dress socks and slipped on my black leather shoes and belt. I tip toed from my closet, avoiding clicking the hard soles of my dress shoes on the tile floor of the bathroom which I feared would wake up my wife and daughter who had crawled into bed with us the night before.

I turned on the light and liked what I saw in the mirror. *If you can't make it... fake it*, I thought to myself. While I wasn't sure of what I was in for throughout this day, at least I felt dressed for the occasion. I fixed my hair and gave myself a wink before snapping off the light and heading for the door.

Driving off the ferry reminded me of the countless times over the previous years that I had driven off the same boat while running my cabinet business, making the same journey I was on today but with a very different purpose. I used to wear work jeans, sneakers and a company golf shirt to meet with my suppliers and do the day's pick-ups. Today I was transformed. Driving my gold Volvo and dressed for success I felt like a new man. And while I wasn't completely comfortable in my new look, I didn't feel like a fraud. I felt like I was becoming the person I wanted to be.

To Get What You Want, You Need to Know What You Want

I stopped at the Starbucks in an affluent part of West Vancouver, knowing that I had more than an hour to kill before having to make my way downtown. I ordered a coffee and the least expensive food item in the counter, still recovering from our family's financial troubles.

"Can I get a medium, medium roast and an oat bar please?" I asked to the bright eyed young lady behind the counter.

"Sorry... so is that a tall medium roast?" she asked, Sharpie in hand, ready to write out the recipe she expected me to present her with on the white paper cup.

"Uh... the one in the middle," I said, embarrassed.

"Grande. It's a grande you're after," she smiled at me... still making me feel like an idiot. "A grande Pike and an Island Oat Bar!" she called out to her co-worker, putting down the Sharpie and punching my order in the till.

We finished our transaction and I took my coffee and little brown bag with the mermaid on it. I grabbed a newspaper and sat in the middle of the coffee shop with a clear vantage point of the young barista and most of the coffee shop. While I had every intention of reading the paper, I didn't read more than a couple of articles the entire time I was there.

Instead, I studied the men and women that came through the door. People who likely followed the same routine every morning... and I was transfixed. At 7:30, there weren't many stay at home moms in the mix. It was predominantly trades people and local workers, there to serve their wealthy clients, and local residents heading into work. It was pretty obvious who the Lexus, Porsches and Mercedes outside belonged to and who drove the old Hondas and pick-up trucks.

I was intrigued by the fact that many of the workers, some of whom (like me) probably couldn't afford the premium price tag of the coffee, put in orders so specific and long winded that the baristas had to re-write the order on a second cup to fit it all in. That's not to say that there weren't people in suits and dresses doing the same thing but there seemed to be a big difference to me. While I found it all a bit ridiculous, I couldn't help surmise that many of the wealthy locals truly understood exactly what it was they wanted and weren't afraid to ask for it. I also got the sense that many of the folks who were obviously out of their element (like me) were putting in crazy orders more for the sake of standing out and for the pleasure of being served by someone else.

My little study was far from scientific, but my deductions were important. I realized that I ordered a simple coffee (dressed up in name to a "Grande Pike Place" mind you) not because it was perfect for me, but because I hadn't taken the time to really figure out what I wanted.

I wasn't sure but something told me that many of the successful, well dressed people in the place had taken the time to decide what it was they want, and simply asked for it. That seemed to be a strategy worth considering for life in general.

I got to the bottom of my cup and made a commitment to myself to start controlling my life by figuring out exactly what I wanted, rather than letting circumstance and random opportunity dictate where I wound up. It was an empowering moment for me that would help me absorb what I would learn over the next two days.

Getting a Handle on the Competition

I arrived in the parking lot under the Hyatt Regency Hotel and reluctantly took the ticket from the automatic dispenser and looked at the $25 a day price tag on the machine. *Seriously?* I headed into the building with a confident stride and tried hard to not look like a scared grade 8 student on his first day at high school, but I couldn't help feel like I was in over my head. I checked the board in the lobby for the event and saw that we were in the Regency Ballroom on the 3rd level.

I stepped on the escalator and overheard the two professionally dressed women in front of me, obviously Realtors® coming to the same event, discussing a deal the younger of the two was working on.

"I just can't believe my clients expect me to cover the spread between their offer and the Seller's bottom line," she said desperately.

"How far apart are they?" the other Realtor® said.

"$5000," was the reply. "I know it's not a lot of money, but it's the principle of it."

$5000 isn't a lot of money?! That was news to me.

The real estate market in Vancouver, while only a 45-minute ferry ride from our community, was as different as night and day. Not only was the type of property being sold vastly different, but housing prices were three to four times higher than ours. I assumed the pressures the 'city' Realtors® faced must have been much greater than ours given the scale of their transactions.

"So what are you going to do?" said the older of the two.

"I'll just swallow the five grand and get the deal done," replied the other. "I'm ready to move on!"

I won't soon forget that escalator ride and the reaction I had to the younger Realtors® submission. I simply couldn't wrap my head around someone "swallowing" $5,000 to get a deal done. What message would that send to the people doing the transaction? What value must they perceive in what she does? What will those clients expect of this Realtor® next time they do a deal? What did it say about her confidence in her ability to negotiate? I asked myself the question: *What would Ryan do?* and I immediately had the answer based on our USP.

"We are a team of caring real estate professionals who help our customers turn their dreams into reality by providing invaluable advice, proven marketing strategies and expert negotiating skills."

Ryan would never have blindly conceded the $5000 reduction in his commissions to get a deal done because he knew the value of the service he was providing.

By just listening in on a couple of sentences, I knew that this seemingly successful Realtor® on the escalator lacked the confidence and skills I longed to attain in this business and that even though she was about to concede a significant amount of money, she was doing so not out of a sense of responsibility to her client, but rather to "get the deal done and move on." It struck me as shallow and unprofessional.

When we reached the top of the first elevator the two ladies turned to the right, apparently seeking a washroom. I carried on to the left and the next escalator in a series that would lead us to the third floor.

I found myself behind a friendly looking couple who wore brass name plates with the logo of the Real Estate Brokerage they worked with 'The Shack Team' in bold print underneath.

"Hi there!" said the bright eyed woman, "I'm Dora Shack and this is my husband Terry. We live and work in Aldergrove."

"Good morning. I'm Alan Stewart from the Sunshine Coast."

"Oh we LOVE the Sunshine Coast!" said Terry a little too enthusiastically. "We have friends with a property on Ruby Lake. It's awesome!"

"Our kids just love it there!" added Dora.

"Yes, it's really world class," I replied.

"Hey, if you ever have people looking to buy or sell in Aldergrove, we would love to help them out and pay you a 25% referral," said Terry as he presented me one of his Shack Team business cards. "We'd be happy to do the same if we come across anyone heading to the Sunshine Coast."

We exchanged cards and as quickly as they had entered my life, they left it, seeing someone they recognized and politely saying good-bye as we reached the second level. While I was at first flattered that they would refer people to me, I also felt that I would likely be forgotten by the Shacks who knew nothing about me. I slid the card into my inside jacket pocket and headed to the third escalator.

I realized that a tall and attractive woman with grey hair and a very polished appearance had been following behind me for both elevator rides. I turned back to her and ask if she were attending the conference.

"I haven't missed one in 6 years," she said with a smile, pointing out her "VIP" status on her name badge that she wore around her neck.

"This is my first," I said, a little unsure of myself. "I'm not exactly sure what to expect."

"You'll love it!" she said. "Donna," She said extending me a hand… with no business card in it.

"Alan," I said, accepting her handshake. "Anything I should know before going in there?"

"Oh, it takes a bit of getting used to the 'rah-rah' at the beginning but you'll find the energy is really contagious."

Donna, sensing the fact that I was a little uptight, invited me to sit with her.

"I'd love to, but I still need to register at the check in desk," I said.

"I'll go and get us some seats. It's first come, first served, so I'll find something as close to centre stage as I can. You get yourself registered and bring us a cup of coffee. Just a little milk in mine," she said.

We were an hour early for the event and hundreds of people were milling about chatting over coffee and tea. I was thankful for having made a connection with someone and looked forward to chatting with Donna once inside. After a few minutes in the "M – S" line, which corresponded to the ticket holder's last name, I was presented with my name badge, just like Donna's but without the "VIP" status and a 1" binder with a large picture of the presenter and the seminar name. "Mr. Real Estate; Real Estate Reinvented!" It was ultra-professional and I was proud to tout it around. I slid the binder under my arm and filled two of the small coffee cups and headed into the ballroom.

I was speechless. It was like a rock concert. Music was pumping and many of the seats near the front were filled already, except for a large section in the middle that was roped off. As I neared the front, I could see that many of the people in the foyer had already claimed their seats by putting their coats and binders on them. It wasn't long before I saw Donna who had found a couple of seats for us quite near the front and next to the roped off section. She waved to me when she saw me.

"Great seats," I said. "Thank you for doing that."

"No, no," she said. "Thank you for the coffee!"

"Why is this centre section roped off?" I asked.

"It's reserved seating for Mr. Real Estate's coaching clients. Mr. Real Estate makes a special point of recognizing his long term clients."

"Is that why you have the "VIP" status?" I asked.

"Exactly. I've been involved in Mr. Real Estate's coaching program for the last 4 years. It took me a couple of years of coming to these events to see the value in it, but after talking to enough people I figured what did I have to lose?"

"So why aren't you sitting in the VIP section?"

"Because I wanted to sit with you," she said, matter of factly. "And besides, these seats are just as good."

I was flattered but I encouraged Donna to go and sit in the seats to which she was entitled but she flatly refused.

We spent the next 40 minutes or so talking about where I had come from, my frustrations and failures in my woodworking business, my wife and kids and my unique experience working with Ryan. Donna seemed absolutely captivated and never once turned the conversation to herself, continuing instead to probe into my life. It wasn't until we started to talk about my relationship with Ryan that she started to add in stories about her life and career in real estate.

"Alan, you have no idea how fortunate you are to have Ryan mentoring you," she told me. "The experience and knowledge he is instilling in you are worth every bit as much as a university education or an apprenticeship with a journeyman."

"The more Realtors® I meet, the more I tend to agree with you," I said honestly. "I didn't go looking for this relationship, but I am sure glad I found it."

It turned out that Donna was one of the top producing Realtors® in her office in Whistler. She had been selling for over 20 years, had taken a stint at managing her office, and then returned to her career, missing the opportunity to serve her clients.

As we got closer to the start time, Donna asked if she could get me another coffee and I gratefully accepted. While it would be my third cup of the day, I had been up for nearly 5 hours and I needed another injection of caffeine to help me get through the day. I reflected on my morning and came to appreciate that the 3 levels of the escalator were good analogies of the kinds of relationships that we can develop with our clients. The ladies' discussion over the $5000 commission reduction on the first escalator reflected how many Realtors® focus on their own needs over the clients and how they treat their clients as just one more transaction for the record books.

The second escalator ride, while much more engaging, was reflective of the superficial "one shot wonder" approach that so many Realtors® hope will drive them towards success. I struggled to remember the name of the couple I had met less than an hour earlier and reached into my pocket to remind myself. "The Shack Team" I said out loud, hoping it would help me remember if I saw them again over the next couple of days.

The third elevator ride and ensuing conversation with Donna would be with me for a lifetime. I felt grateful to have a friend through the conference and someone I knew I could count on if I even needed to refer someone buying or selling in Whistler. This was the ultimate kind of relationship to strive for, and while it took the two of us nearly an hour to get to know one another, the future spin offs for both of us far outweighed any hourly rate we could ever expect to charge. That hour with Donna would have a profound effect on both of us in the coming months.

Super Star

As Donna returned with our coffee, the music volume increased significantly and a heavy dance beat engulfed us.

"Ladies and Gentlemen," said the emcee who was nowhere to be seen, "Mr. Real Estate will be coming to the stage in five minutes. Please return to your seats immediately. Again, Mr. Real Estate will be joining us in only five minutes. Please return to your seats immediately."

The lights dimmed slightly and a spotlight started circling the crowd. The massive display screens began showing photos of Mr. Real Estate and his coaching clients receiving all kinds of awards and accolades, standing atop massive yachts and mountain peaks, racing the streets in fast cars and helping feed children in third world countries. The people in the VIP section began to clap their hands to the beat of the music which I would come to appreciate was Mr. Real Estate's theme song and it wasn't long before the rest of crowd started to join in.

People flooded through the doors from the foyer and made their way into their seats clapping all the while. I started to feel REALLY out of place.

"I told you the rah-rah took a little getting used to!" Donna yelled into my ear, clapping as hard as anyone else.

I timidly clapped, fearing a lynching if I kept my hands at my side. "This is unbelievable," I said.

Just then the curtains drew back and a well-dressed man came on stage with the microphone held high over his head, clapping with the rhythm of the audience. This was not Mr. Real Estate. Was this the opening act? I was not prepared for anything like this but continued clapping all the same.

"Ladies and Gentlemen," he said, obviously the voice of the emcee that had announced Mr. Real Estate's pending arrival five minutes earlier, "are you ready to make some money?"

"Ohhhhh Ya!" screamed the crowd in unison.

"Are you ready to make some changes in your life?"

"Ohhhhh Ya!" the crowd cheered again.

"Are you ready to wake up your business!?"

"Ohhhhh Ya!" This time I mouthed the words, not to be seen as outcast.

"Are you ready to take you career to a whole new level?"

"Ohhhhh Ya!" I admit, I joined the crowd at this point.

"Then let's give it up for the man whose mission it is to help you build the life of your dreams! The One. The Only. Mr. Mr. Real Estate!!!!"

The lights dimmed completely and the spotlights all swung around to focus on the centre of the rear curtains, and like magic Mr. Mr. Real Estate in all his glory bound onto the stage and embraced the emcee before he was handed the microphone. The crowd roared and then joined Mr. Real Estate as he continued the rhythmic clapping as he bounced across the stage encouraging everyone to join in. The energy was electric and the effect unarguable. It was a rush, even though I did my best to try and keep from getting swept up in the moment.

We spent the next two days going through the workbook we had been given. We developed a business plan for the coming year based on some straightforward questions outlined on just a couple sheets of paper, simplifying the task to its most rudimentary elements

(See Appendix B: Goal Setting and Annual Business Plan)

CHAPTER 4

WORKING WITH BUYERS

My first client was a potential buyer from Toronto who had been corresponding with Ryan for months. He was planning a trip to our community in the hopes of securing a West Coast waterfront retreat. Until the day before his arrival I had no idea that he also happened to be the number one commercial Realtor® in Toronto. *Pressure.*

"Welcome Mr. Dobbs," said Ryan as the buyer and his wife walked through the office door on a bright sunny afternoon. "After communicating so long by email it is really great to finally meet you in person."

"I can hardly believe we are here Ryan. It's great to finally meet you in the flesh."

"Alan, please meet Mr. Wayne Dobbs," Ryan said as Mr. Dobbs turned his attention to me. "It's hard to believe, but Mr. Dobbs found our little team on the internet while sitting in his home office in Toronto, and three months later, here he is... over 4000 kilometres from home... right here in our little office."

"Very nice to meet you Mr. Dobbs," I said as I extended a hand. "The internet certainly has shrunk our world, hasn't it?"

"Pleasure to meet you as well Alan. Please call me Wayne," he said, accepting my hand. "Ryan tells me that you are going to be our tour guide for the next few days which we're thankful for. While the world may be smaller, I still struggle with directions!"

"I'll do my best! I've previewed all the properties on your list, and added a couple that Ryan and I thought may be of interest."

"Wayne," Ryan injected, "as you know Alan is new to the business. While he may not know the answer to all your questions, rest assured that he will be taking notes throughout the day and we'll meet each evening to discuss any concerns you may have."

"That's great Ryan. I'm pretty sure I'll know what we're after when I see it."

"I hope so!" I added. "Now Wayne, I'm not sure how it works in Ontario, but in British Columbia there are a few forms I have to review with you to explain what you can expect from me before we get started… then we'll be ready to hit the road first thing in the morning. Can we take a minute to do that now?"

"Sure thing Alan."

We spent the next couple of days walking acreages and lots and looking at homes. I was surprised at how many times I had to take notes, not knowing the answer to so many of his questions: setbacks for buildings from the waterfront, setbacks from side property lines, costs of installing septic systems and delivering water, construction costs, tax rates, building restrictions, measurement conversions, covenants and easements…. and general questions about area population, access to amenities, referrals to different contractors, building inspectors, architects, and arborists. If my confidence level was an 8 out of 10 when we ventured out in the morning, it was probably a 3 by the time we returned to the office. It was obvious that I hadn't learned everything I needed to know.

Ryan had spent hours corresponding with Mr. Dobbs before his arrival. I had spent 5 hours preparing for their visit and a total of 20 hours in the two days we worked together, along with nearly a tank of gas and some significant wear and tear on my car as we drove driveways that were only suitable for 4x4's. And while we enjoyed our time together and shared many laughs, Mr. Dobbs and his wife didn't buy anything that week. In fact, they didn't buy anything in our community at all; rather they wound up buying a property in another seaside community that had direct flights from Toronto. Didn't they know that would be important before coming? Why didn't Ryan or I think to ask THAT question!?

While I was disappointed that the hard work hadn't turned into a sale or a paycheque, I was thankful for the opportunity to learn the answers to the many questions that Mr. Dobbs asked me. Over time, I learned that no one could have known the answer to all the questions he set out. While my level of knowledge about contractors, costs and bylaws would grow with experience, a professional Realtor® need never be embarrassed about having to find information about properties they don't have listed for sale.

Every situation is different and offers us a unique opportunity to learn. Even when touring properties. If we aren't learning about the product, we are learning about our clients. If we aren't learning about our clients, we're learning about the style of other Realtors®. Failing that, there is always room to learn something about ourselves. Ryan taught me to ask "What is the lesson in this?" whenever I was faced with a problem or a challenge. It is an important question that successful people ask themselves regularly. And then they add the answer to their experience arsenal.

After we received the news that Mr. Dobbs had purchased in another community through a different Realtor®, I asked Ryan about what we could have done differently to qualify our buyers.

"It's a fine line Alan, but I have a list of basic criteria a client has to meet before we head out to look at properties. I'll provide a lot of information and answer a lot of questions for just about anybody when asked on the phone or online, but before I'll spend time with them in the car looking at properties they have to pass a pretty basic checklist."

"So did Mr. Dobbs pass your test?" I asked.

"Yes... but we can't win them all. I asked the Dobbs if they had any problem with using the ferry system or float plane service to get to their recreation property and they claimed not. I provided them with a link to the ferry schedule and floatplane company's website and explained the reservation process for both services. They have friends here, and assured me they were comfortable with the transportation issues."

"I guess it's a numbers game then?" I asked. "I'll just have to keep running with buyers... until I find one that will buy!"

"You're right, it is a numbers game. But fortunately we have lots of opportunity to stack the deck in our favour. Far too many agents do nothing to qualify their clients," Ryan responded. "I'm cautious about over qualifying buyers and running the risk of not being able to help someone that is sincere and capable of buying."

"How would that happen?"

"You'll find that no matter how open and honest you are, some people simply refuse to open up until they have been able to build a relationship with you. They may even lie to you in order to avoid 'the sales pitch.' Maybe you've even found yourself stretching the truth in a store where the commission salespeople seem to be pouncing on you?"

"Sure, that makes sense," I replied. "So how do we decide who we're going to work with and who we're not going to invest time in?"

"We invest time in everyone," he said without pausing. "But how much time... and what resources we invest is the decision we have to make. Everyone deserves our attention, but we have to ensure we don't waste our time, and theirs, by ensuring that they are capable and sincere. Here's a worksheet I've used for years to do just that."

Buyer Worksheet

(See Appendix C: Buyer Worksheet)

How long have you been looking for a home?	
What neighbourhoods are you interested in exploring?	
What is it about these neighbourhoods that makes them interesting?	*Schools, parks, proximity to work,....*
Do you have friends or family in the neighbourhood?	*Who?...*

Do you have a clear picture in your mind of what your perfect home would look like?	*Can you describe it? How many bedrooms and baths? Specific features?...*
Have you seen any specific homes that you like? Can you describe them for me?	*Pay attention to benefits over features...*
How soon would you like to move in?	
Do you need to sell an existing home to buy the next one?	
Are you working with any other Real Estate Agents in looking for a home?	*If not, may I prepare a complimentary CMA?...*
What price range are you considering? Have you been prequalified by a financial institution?	

How much are you prepared to pay monthly on your mortgage?	
How much do you intend to put towards the down payment?	
Are there any other people who need to see the home before you make a decision to buy?	
Would be ready to make an offer on a house today if we were able to find the PERFECT home for you?	*If not, why not?...*
What is the best way to reach you in the event that a suitable property comes on the market?	
Are there any other questions or concerns you have?	

My First Sale: Some come easy... some come hard.

While I would have much preferred selling a multi-million-dollar waterfront home to Mr. Dobbs, my first actual sale was to a young janitor at our local school. The property that he was interested in was the cheapest listing in the neighbourhood, an old ramshackle home that was owned by a wealthy Vancouver business person and which was being rented out to a young couple with little resources and even less interest in keeping the house presentable.

Tenanted properties can be the most challenging to sell. The tenants are often frustrated with the process, having to prepare for showings and have complete strangers go through their house, knowing that when it sells there is a very good chance they will be evicted. I had shown the house a number of times and had become friendly with the young tenants, and even though it wasn't one of Ryan's listings, I encouraged them to keep the house tidy in hopes of having an investor purchase it who would keep them on.

When Greg, the custodian, called to make an arrangement to view the property he told me that he was looking at it as a place for him to live and that it was the only property that met his criteria and was in a price range he felt he could afford.

"Okay Greg, I'll make arrangements to view the home on Thursday after work, but before I do I need to ask you a few questions," I said.

"Like what?" he asked.

"Well, the Seller's agent has told us that he can only show the property to prequalified buyers. Have you spoken to the bank about your ability to secure financing for a home in this price range?"

"Well, no. But I've got about 25% to put down on the home. Isn't that enough?" he asked.

"That's certainly a great start Greg, but before we are able to view the house I'll need to have you speak to your banker about being qualified for a mortgage. If you don't have a banker, I'd be happy to give you a list of folks that could help you out."

"That's okay. I'll make an appointment with my bank right now," Greg replied. "Anything else?"

"Yes, a few more things I need to ask over the phone Greg," I replied. "Before we assist our clients in showing them properties, we have a brief questionnaire that we complete to ensure our clients are in the strongest position to move forward when they find the right property. Not only does it allow us to make sure our clients aren't disappointed by looking at properties outside of their price range, but it also helps us negotiate the best possible price for them when we are able to tell the Seller's that our clients have been pre-qualified and that they are in a position to buy. I'm sure if you were selling your home, you would want to be sure the buyers that were looking at your home were actually in a position to buy."

"Sounds fair," Greg said. "Shoot."

I went through Ryan's Buyer Checklist and the Pre Qualification Worksheet and was satisfied that his responses met Ryan's criteria.

Buyer Checklist / Information Sheet

Source		Date		
Name (1)		Cell		☐Text OK
email		Other		
Name (2)		Cell		☐Text OK
email		Other		
Address				
Address 2				
Price Range		Move Date		
Motivation	☐ L ☐ M ☐ H ☐ URGENT!	Type	☐Detached ☐ Attached ☐ Multi ☐ Land	
Pets		# Family		
Needs				
Wants				

Buyer Provided / Acknowledged	To Do Upon Accepted Offer
Agency Brochure (signed and in file)	Transaction Record Sheet
Exclusive Buyer's Agency Agreement	Offer & Deposit to Office
Home Buyer's Guide	Contract sent to lender
Current Market Information Graph	Purchaser's S.I.N.'s
Current Listings	Deposit Rec'd (copy to Listing Agent)
First Time Buyers Exemption	Mortgage Approved
RRSP Downpayment Info	Bylaws & Financials(Strata) subject removal date:
5% Downpayment Recommendation	Title, Inspection, and other subject removal date:
Mortgage Broker Referral	FINTRAC Identification
Blank Contract for review	Lawyers Names (Buyer / Seller)

(See Appendix D: Buyer Checklist/Information Sheet)

"Finally Greg, I've been through this particular home a number of times, and the last time I was there I noticed some issues with what I think might be dry-rot and mold that likely needs to be addressed," I said. "The tenants are aware of the situation, as is the Seller's agent, but we need to get some more information."

"So is it going to fall down?" Greg asked, concerned.

"I don't think it's going to fall down Greg," I said with a smile, "but it's important that you get some professional advice before we move too far forward. What I'd like to do is have a contractor join us at the house on Thursday to give you, and I, some sense of what the cost of repairs might be. Would that be OK?"

"Of course. Thanks for doing that."

"No problem Greg. Give me a call as soon as you know about the financing and I'll set up the showing. I'm going to email you a list of contractors in the area that might be able to help and you can let me know which one you'd like me to call."

I was learning. I was learning the value of not wasting the time of the Seller, the tenants and myself by being sure that the people I was working with were not only sincere in their interest to buy, but that had done as much homework as possible. Having Greg get pre-qualified not only minimized the potential frustration of him not being able to purchase, but it also strengthened his negotiating position in the event that he wanted to put in an offer. As it turns out, it also opened up more opportunities for Greg as he qualified for a much more substantial mortgage than he would need for this property.

"Alan, it's Greg," was the response to me answering my cell phone. "The bank says I'm fine to purchase the house, so long as we can get a satisfactory appraisal."

"That's great news Greg. I've already tentatively set up the meeting with the Contractor you asked that I call; I just need to make arrangements with the listing Realtor® and the tenants. Unless you hear back from me, let's meet at my office on Thursday at 3:30 and we'll head over together."

"Perfect. I'll see you then," Greg said excitedly.

On Thursday afternoon we pulled up the dirt driveway and found the tenants home, but making their way out the door. I introduced Greg to them both and they were quick to point out to him all the problems with the home.

"Alan thinks he found dry-rot in the living room and we've been coughing a lot in there. We think there might be mold. And the dishwasher has been leaking for a long time so the floor in the kitchen is kind of spongy," said the husband.

"Oh, and don't forget that our cat and her new kittens are locked in the far bedroom. We've put a pad-lock on there, so you can't go into that room," said the wife.

A pad-lock? I thought. *Must be some kind of cat!* Although our spider senses were tingling, Greg and I were anxious to have the couple leave and so we didn't argue accessing the bedroom.

The young couple headed out the door and I assured them we would be done in an hour. We started to make our way through the various rooms of the house and it wasn't long before the contractor arrived.

Tom was a burly young guy who had done a fair amount of renovation work in the past for Ryan. Ryan was pleased when Greg chose Tom too and he suggested that he would give us practical advice and that he would be the right guy for Greg to talk to, knowing that we would have to keep costs down on any renovation. Tom joined us on the tour and started making notes as we walked from room to room.

"Tom, here is the spot on the window sill that I thought might be rotten?"

Tom pushed his pen into the window sill and it went through it as if it were a marshmallow. "Yup. That's an issue for sure," he said, looking up to the top of the window frame. "You can see that water has been coming down here for a long time. We'll have to have a look at it from outside, but it's probably a flashing issue."

Tom returned to his notepad and jotted something down. "We won't know how big of a deal it is until we can open up the wall and have a look."

We carried on into the kitchen for some more bad news, which was followed with more disheartening insights about the plumbing in the bathroom and the ventilation in the attic. I kept an eye on Greg, who seemed to be getting paler as the tour went on. This was not going well and the idea of a paycheque seemed to be slipping away again.

As a final part of the interior inspection, Tom opened the hatch to the crawl space and went in. I had looked in the crawl space before and hadn't noticed anything too suspicious, but Tom came back up with a grin on his face.

"Did you say this place was rented?" Tom asked.

"Yes," I replied. "Why do you ask?"

"Looks like they've got green thumbs," Tom said. "Come have a look."

I took the flashlight from Tom's outstretched hand and peered down into the crawlspace. *Oh.*

I passed the flashlight to Greg who looked down and saw the 4 marijuana plants that were stowed away in the crawlspace.

"Doesn't look like they are growing them there, just hid them while we were doing the tour," Tom said. "It does make me wonder what's going on in that locked room, however."

With Greg at his palest shade yet, we decided to go outside to inspect the perimeter of the house and I wondered if we weren't wasting our time. I was too afraid to ask Greg how he was feeling. By this point Tom and Greg were becoming more familiar with each other and comfortable. I fell in behind them as Tom explained what he felt was a reasonable lifespan on the roof and what things he thought needed to be addressed right away.

As they turned their attention to the sewer system, or lack thereof, I asked if it would be OK for me to take a phone call from the office. I stepped away from their conversation and towards my car. I turned back to look at Tom who was pointing to the sewer outflow pipe coming from the kitchen and indicating where he thought the septic tank might be when all of the sudden, like a bad magic trick, Greg shrunk to half his previous height - his head now at Tom's waist level.

Tom and I looked down at Greg, and back at each other, and back at Greg... all of us in a state of confusion. The colour that had drained from Greg's face returned for a moment when he realized he wasn't hurt and then retreated to near white as we realized what had happened. Greg had fallen through the rotten sheet of plywood atop the septic tank and was now waist deep in the tenant's sewage. And I was his ride home. This day couldn't get any worse.

After hosing off Greg as best we could, we parted company with Tom and Greg offered to walk back to the office. "Not on your life!" I told him. I was thankful for the leather seats in my old Volvo, knowing that I'd need to disinfect them when I got home.

We got back to the office and Greg told me he'd call me later to discuss.

"Of course Greg," I said. "You've got a lot to think about. Again, I'm so sorry for what happened and I understand if you've lost interest in the house."

Another day wasted, I suspected. I called the Seller's agent to let him know about the events of the afternoon and some of the things we had found out about the property. While he couldn't resist chuckling about my description of Greg's fall into the septic tank, he was obviously disappointed and confided in me that the seller was thinking of tearing the place down and just selling the land, knowing that it would take a miracle to find someone willing to buy the house in its current condition.

When Greg called me that evening, I was surprised by his upbeat tone.

"Alan. I've decided I want to make an offer on the property," he said.

"Really?" I responded... unable to catch myself! "That's great, Greg. I'm really glad that Tom was able to join us so that you can move forward without any big surprises."

"You know what Alan?" he asked. "If Tom weren't there, I never would have considered putting in an offer. The dry-rot alone probably would have been enough to scare me off. But I'm confident in Tom and when I called him just now, we talked about all the potential costs and how long it would take to do the work. If I can get the house for the right price, I think this can be a really good solution for me."

Shocking. If the inspection wasn't the nail in the coffin, I was sure falling into a tank of excrement would have sealed the fate of this deal. But I learned that day that there is a buyer for every home. It may take some time to find them, but they are out there. And as a salesperson and consultant, it isn't my job to assume tastes or risk tolerance for my clients. Rather, it's my job to provide all the information I possibly can so that they can make their own decisions.

Preparing Offers

In the beginning, I would work closely with buyers until they were ready to prepare an offer on a property, at which time, Ryan would re-enter the picture and assist us in preparing the paperwork. Ryan never liked to refer to contracts as anything other than "paperwork," fearing the word contract might scare people from moving forward.

I appreciated the many systems that Ryan had developed over his career, which included his method for preparing contracts.

Whenever possible, we would have our clients come to our office. Not only was it was much more efficient to prepare paperwork there, with access to all the computers, printers, photocopiers and information we may need, but as a professional Ryan wanted to establish the same relationship with his clients that they may have with their Lawyer or Notary.

"Nobody expects house calls from their Lawyer, at least not without adding to the cost of the service." Ryan would say, and as a professional Ryan knew his time was best served by having clients come to him. No drive time. No risk of wasted time waiting for clients to show up at a meeting. If a client was delayed, Ryan was able to carry on with his other business until they arrived. And of course, having the meeting conducted in the Ryan's office, on HIS waterfront property, had a psychological effect on the client and undoubtedly increased his influence over their decisions.

As an "expert," Ryan believed that part of the reason he was paid was to give good and informed advice on negotiating strategies and to help his clients get the best value when buying or selling a property. But too often, he had been frustrated with people who operated from a strictly emotional position, and getting them into his office, his arena, allowed him to draw their attention back to the financial decision they were undertaking.

I arranged for Greg to come and meet us at the office on the evening he called wanting to make an offer. Ryan and I agreed to meet one half hour before Greg arrived, and I assumed we would use that time to prepare the necessary forms necessary. However, when I arrived, Ryan was already there, pouring boiled water into the kettle for a fresh pot of tea. I was greeted with a warm squeeze on the shoulder and congratulations for getting the deal to this stage.

"Trust me, Ryan," I chimed in. "Whatever could have gone wrong on this deal, already has. I'd be surprised if it were possible for there to be any more bumps in the road!"

"Alan, you'll find that some deals come easy... and some come hard. It's just the nature of the business," he assured me. "Let's take a walk down to the beach and you can tell me all about it."

"Don't we need to get things together for Greg?" I asked.

"I always have Kim keep a half dozen folders filled with all the forms I need for preparing offers ready to go, and I've put one of those on the meeting table for us to review with Greg. The rest of the information we'll key into the computer after meeting with Greg and understanding what the offer needs to reflect. Now come on, the tea will be ready by the time we're back."

I looked over and saw the green file folder with white label on the circular table, with Greg's name and the address of the property written neatly with a fine black Sharpie on a crisp white label on the file folder's tab. On top of it were two black pens, one for Greg and one for Ryan.

We meandered along the trail to Ryan's dock, with both of us laughing almost to the point of tears by the time I finished explaining the events of the day to him. Never in his 12 years of selling real estate had Ryan ever heard of such a fiasco.

"And he still wants to write an offer?" Ryan asked, wiping his eyes. "That's unbelievable!"

"I know. I was shocked, but like you say… there's a buyer for every property!"

"And was Greg hurt in the fall?"

"Other than his pride? I don't think so. To be honest… I was too embarrassed about the whole situation to even ask when he called me tonight."

"Alan, remember that none of this was your doing," he reassured me. "There is a temptation for people to run from situations and hide from problems. But know this, any problem you run from only gets bigger. If you want to be a success, you have to be a hero. You have to have the courage and confidence to face situations head on. If you have something to apologize for… then apologize. But if something goes sideways and you've done your best, take the high road and ask the questions that need to be asked or do the things that need to be done."

"You're right," I admitted. "The other day in the grocery store, I saw an old client from the cabinet shop that didn't like the kitchen we installed… even though it was exactly what she asked for. Rather than risk a confrontation, I backed out of the aisle before she could see me."

"Was there anything you could have done to have helped her make a better decision in her choice of cabinets?" Ryan asked.

"I knew you were going to ask that!" I sighed. "She hated the way the wood finish looked with her slate flooring, and maybe I should have had her approve a sample of the finished door in her house so she could have checked how it looked with the flooring before we went ahead and built them all. But..."

"Butts are for cigarettes Alan," he interrupted. "At the end of the day, you've got an unhappy client who is going to think a certain way about you every time she walks into that kitchen. Is there anything you could do to resolve the situation?"

"I could replace all her kitchen doors... but that would cost thousands of dollars!"

"Is she prepared to pay for new doors?" he asked.

"No way. She was tight from the get go and ground me down on every aspect of the job. It cost me money to get out of there."

"Have you asked her? I know if it were me, I'd rather spend the money to have my home look the way I want than have to live with something I don't like."

I agreed to have the conversation with my old client to see if there was anything I could do.

Ryan changed the subject and told me about his plans for a new dock that would replace the old grey cedar one we stood on, and then we made our way back up to the house in time to see Greg's old blue pick-up truck pull into the driveway.

We made our way over to the truck, shaking Greg's hand as Ryan deftly dealt with the elephant in the room, the fall from earlier in the day.

"Greg, Alan told me about what happened earlier today and I want you to know I appreciate how you must have felt. I had a similar experience when I was in the Navy... but I'll refrain from sharing the gory details, just as I am sure you would prefer not to discuss the matter of the septic tank any further."

"Thank you for that Ryan," Greg replied. "Like they say, whatever doesn't kill you makes you stronger! I've got a doctor's appointment lined up for tomorrow just to be safe."

We all made our way into the office and Ryan directed us both to the meeting table.

"Greg, what do you take in your tea?" Ryan asked.

"Just a little milk, thanks."

Ryan made us all tea and then extracted a beautiful, untouched homemade apple pie from the fridge.

"My wife made this pie this morning after picking the apples off the tree in the backyard. I figured you both could use a piece!"

We spent the better part of 15 minutes enjoying the pie and talking about the inspection at the house. Greg had compiled a list of the things we learned about the house from Tom and conservative estimates of what it might cost to remedy each of them. Ryan nodded as he went through the list and made a few notes on a separate sheet of paper.

"I'm really pleased that you and Alan agreed to have Tom go through the house with you in advance of getting an offer put together," Ryan commented. "Too often we go through a negotiation only having to go back to the drawing board when things like this come to light."

We then went through each item on Greg's list, deciding whether or not the deficiency should reasonably be expected in a house of this age, and whether or not we wanted to use it as a negotiating point."

"It's important to remember Greg that you aren't buying a new home here," Ryan injected. "If this were a new home, we would expect things to be in "as new" condition, but we can't expect the seller to provide you with more than he is offering for sale. Take the roof for example. While Tom suggests it has 5-10 years left in its useful life, the Seller already factored that into his listing price. It's the same thing for the hot water tank. Replacing hot water tanks is a maintenance issue, and while the one in the home may be nearing the end of its useful life, it's not leaking and it's operating just fine."

"I understand what you're saying, but these are all costs that I'm going to have to incur in the next 5-10 years," Greg replied. "It seems to me that the Seller should bear some of that expense."

"Welcome to the world of being a homeowner Greg," Ryan smiled. "I'm sure the Seller would gladly bear some of the expense if the offer is right, particularly when we know he's considering tearing the house down. Our job is to try and help you both come to terms on a fair price. Now can we agree that you will factor the estimated costs of handling the dry-rot and other unforeseen costs into your offer, but that we won't look to the Seller to pay for the costs of a new roof and hot water tank?"

"That's fair," conceded Greg.

We spent the next 15 minutes analysing other comparable sales to help Greg come to a reasonable offering amount after factoring in the costs of repairs, and determining the dates for completion and possession, after having the Seller evict the current tenants with the required notice. Then we moved on to what subjects needed to be addressed.

Ryan led in, "Okay Greg, this is a great start. Now we know that you have been preapproved for more than this amount, but the financing is still subject to the bank receiving a satisfactory appraisal on the property's value, so I'm going to suggest that we include a subject to that effect."

"What do you mean by a subject?" asked Greg, who looked a little surprised that there was more to consider after coming to an offering price.

Having completed my course, and being confident with the answer, I chimed in, "Greg, while some offers are "unconditional," most offers in this kind of market include subjects, or conditions, for the buyers to allow them to ensure they are getting what they are bargaining for."

"That make sense," Greg nodded.

"Sellers might expect to see offers that are subject to the buyer securing financing, contracting for and receiving a satisfactory building inspection and reviewing and approving the title search to make sure there are no surprises," I continued.

"But we've done a building inspection with Tom and we've already lined up our financing."

"We've had Tom do an inspection, but he's not a certified inspector. I would still encourage you to hire a certified home inspector, who will conduct an even more thorough analysis of the condition of the home and provide you with a written report on his findings. That's likely going to cost you around $500, but it's money well spent for peace of mind. I'd also encourage you to have the septic system inspected by a qualified professional. All we know at the moment is that the lid is rotten! That's another cost, but again, it could prove to be an expensive problem down the road. If it's not functioning correctly, we can hope to look to the Seller to help bear the cost of repair."

"Do you agree Ryan?" Greg asked, looking over to my advisor.

"Absolutely Greg. We've already reviewed the title search, and there are no charges on title that would be of any concern. Alan can provide you with a list of building inspectors you can speak with and your bank will line up the appraisal. But we would be remiss in not recommending you make your offer conditional to these things. "

"Alright, if you don't think it's going to screw up the offer," conceded Greg. "We are going in well below his asking price, and I don't want to offend the Seller."

"I don't see any risk here Greg. Now are there any other concerns you need to address or information you need to have before you would be prepared to purchase the property?"

"Well, I'd sure feel better if I could have my parents have a look at the property. Do you think we could make that happen?"

Having heard Ryan go through this question with another buyer, I chimed in with what I hoped was a reasonable solution. "Greg, our advice is not to move forward with an offer until you are sure you want to buy this property. If you're convinced that this is the property for you, and are wanting some confirmation from your folks, I'd recommend that we bring them along for the inspection. But if you aren't sure that this is the home for you, perhaps we should step back from the offer process until you know you want it to avoid spending money on the inspections."

"Nope. This is my place... I can feel it," he said confidently. "Let's make the offer and I'll bring my parents through when we are doing the inspection."

"That's great Greg," said Ryan. "It's going to take me half an hour or so to prepare all the paperwork for your signature and initials, so why don't you and Alan take that time to go through the title search and the documentation while I go to work on the computer?"

Ryan excused himself from the table, taking the file and notes with him. Greg and I started going through all the elements of the title search, and while I had to interrupt Ryan a couple of times for clarification, for the most part I understood and was able to communicate the "legalese" to Greg without losing his attention.

In about 20 minutes, 10 minutes shy of his estimate, the printer started to whir and soon after Ryan returned with about 15 pages that needed to be approved and signed by Greg. Ten minutes later we were all done, and ready to submit the offer. Greg left the office knowing that we wouldn't likely speak again until the morning, as we agreed that if we hadn't heard anything by 9:00pm, we would deal with it tomorrow.

"Good job Alan." said Ryan.

"I didn't really do much. I hope I didn't go too far in making the suggestions I did?"

Ryan put a reassuring hand on my shoulder. "You did everything just right. I was really pleased to see that you had Greg's best interests at heart. While it's easy to push for the sale, the way you are going to build a lifelong career in this business, or any other, is to care for your clients. That way, they'll be back... and they'll send their friends."

Preparing for the Offer Presentation

It was pushing 8:30 p.m. and Ryan had a policy of not contacting other Realtors® after 9 o'clock. "Alan, I want you to call the listing agent and let him know that we have an offer we'd like to present. At this stage of the game, we're not looking to provide any information on the offer; rather, we just want to find out when we can present it to the Seller."

I referred to the data sheet for the property, turned on the speaker phone so Ryan could listen in, and dialed the number for the listing agent whom I had given the relatively bad news about the initial inspection earlier.

"Hello Brad. Sorry for calling at this late hour," I started, "but I have an offer for your client's consideration on the Lake Rd. property. Can you tell me when we can present it to your Seller?"

"Really!?" said Brad... unable to catch himself. "That's great news Alan. I thought the inspection didn't go so well?"

"The estimates for correcting some of the bigger issues were a lot less than our client expected, so it turned out to be a good thing to do a preliminary assessment. Our offer will still be subject to an inspection, but I'm pleased the buyer is heading into the negotiations with his eyes open."

"You bet," agreed Brad. "Tell me what the offer is and I'll run it by my Seller. We can look after the paperwork in the morning."

I stumbled, not wanting to offend Brad who just asked me to do the exact opposite of what Ryan and every other esteemed professional has told me to do. "I'm sorry Brad, but I've been given explicit instructions to present the offer in person. Is there a time we can get together?"

"Oh, that's going to be a problem. My Seller is in Vancouver and has asked that any offers be emailed to him for review."

"Well that is a problem. Hang on a second for me Brad."

I hit the mute button on the phone and looked to Ryan for advice. "We can't always negotiate on our terms, but we owe it Greg to do the best we can. Ask him if we can at least have a three-way telephone conversation with the Seller to review the offer."

"Brad, thanks for holding. Listen, I think we can find a compromise here. There are parts of the offer that really demand explanation, but if your Seller is amenable I'd like to coordinate a three-way telephone call with you both at 8:45 tomorrow morning. I'll email you both the offer once we're all on the line and then leave you both to discuss it. Can you see if you can arrange that?"

"Sure Alan. If you don't hear back from me in the next 10 minutes, just assume we are on for 8:45am tomorrow. Cheers."

Ryan stood up and headed over to the coat rack to put on his jacket. "Well done my boy. That's as good as we're going to get. I'll see you here at 8:30 unless I hear from you. Sleep tight."

He slid out the door, knowing that I would wait out the 10 minutes and lock up to his satisfaction. It felt good to be trusted. It felt good to gain the confidence of someone I respected so much.

Presenting the Offer

I didn't sleep well that night. Even though it was a relatively inexpensive property, a deal like this would likely pay me more than $2000. For a couple of day's work, that was big money for me. While I didn't consider the fact that it also would have to cover all the days I worked for the other 10 or so buyers I had taken out to show properties, it was a healthy start.

At 6:37am, not able to wait for the 7:00am alarm I had set, I popped out of bed and took the dog for a walk around the block. The dog was pleased with the unusual event and the exercise helped relieve some of the stress I was under. I had butterflies in my stomach, just like the day of a big game in high school football. But unlike football, my teammates wouldn't be with me on this day. Today, I had the responsibility of taking care of a really big deal for Greg... and me, with only the assistance of Ryan on the sidelines.

I showered, shaved and dressed and headed into the office at 7:45am, wanting to impress Ryan by having coffee ready on his arrival. As I pulled in the driveway, however, Ryan's car was already in its usual spot.

"What are you doing in so early?" he asked.

"I was about to ask you the same thing."

"I'm an early bird," he said. "I always like to get into the office by 6:30 to get ready for the day. By the time 9:00 rolls around and you and Kim come in, it gets too busy to take care of the important stuff."

"Important stuff? You're always doing important stuff," I scoffed.

"No, no. I don't mean the urgent stuff... the stuff we have to attend to when the phone rings. I mean the IMPORTANT stuff. Stuff like improving our systems and figuring out where we are going with things."

"And getting the coffee going for us?" I laughed.

"Yes, that too!"

I poured a cup of the hour old coffee and headed over to the meeting table to get ready for my big call. I went to the file folder holder on the wall and retrieved Greg's file from the night before. There were three large sections to the file holder each with a type set label:

1. Current Buyers

2. Offers in Process

3. Pending Deals

Ryan had established a colour coded system for dealing with the different file types that circulated around the office. Listing folders were blue. Buyers' folders were red. Offers for either one of our buyers or one of our listings were put in green files. Green, like the colour of money. If we had a buyer involved, the red file was temporarily placed in the green file to keep them together.

For us, a green file was a potential paycheque and required a lot of attention. If a file was in the Offers in Process section, we all paid attention to it so that we never dropped the ball but each file was ultimately the responsibility of Ryan or myself. Offers that Ryan was working with were marked with a bright purple dot on the label. Offers that I was working with were marked with a bright orange dot. Systems.

Once an offer had been accepted, it was moved into the Pending Deals section of the file holder. Moving a file from the Offers in Process section to the Pending Deals section was a big deal, and something we celebrated by ringing a brass ship's bell hanging beside the door. If we could get a deal together, we really felt we had done our job because from that point on, when a deal fell apart it was rarely something that we could prevent. While we would move mountains to try and deal with financing problems, appraisal and bad building inspections, these things were, for the most part, out of our control.

In front of me was Greg's green file, which held all the pertinent forms for making our offer, the notes from our building inspection, a loose-leaf sheet with Tom's estimates that Greg had given me over the phone, and the documents that Brad had sent us to review. Also tucked into the green offer file was Greg's red file which included the information sheet I had filled out for him early in our relationship, a signed Agency Brochure, and the notes I had taken during our meeting with Ryan the night before.

Ryan was at his desk, reviewing a notebook that looked like it had been with him for a long time. I fired up my laptop computer and headed for the scanner attached to Kim's computer, and sent a copy of the offer to myself. It was 8:15am.

"Do you mind if I ask you a couple of questions before calling Brad with the offer?" I said, interrupting him.

"Not at all, but it will have to wait until 8:30. I make a habit of committing my first 2 hours a day to truly important stuff Alan," he replied politely. Ryan reached into his briefcase and pulled out a copy of Stephen Covey's book, Seven Habits of Highly Effective People. Throwing it to me he said, "Check out page 151" he said, "and keep the book."

I thumbed the book open and was immediately captivated by the graph which noted four quadrants that people spent time in. Ryan had drafted a real estate related graph on a piece of looseleaf paper stuck in between the pages.

Ryan's 4 Q's	Urgent	Not Urgent
Important	Quadrant 1 • Crisis • Listing Presentation • Showings	Quadrant 2 (BE HERE!) • Relationship Building • Planning • Personal Growth • R & R
Not Important	Quadrant 3 • Interruptions • some emails, calls, meetings	Quadrant 4 • Facebook • Trivia / "busywork" • some calls and emails

I spent the next 15 minutes skimming through the book that Ryan had marked up over the years and obviously referred to like a holy text. I was moved that he would offer it to me.

At 8:30am, Ryan's watch beeped and he snapped out of what appeared to be a trance, allowing him to shift gears into the urgent and time sensitive world of my offer! "Alright, shoot."

"Shoot?" I ask.

"Your questions. Didn't you say you had a couple for me?"

"Oh right. I'm a little concerned about speaking directly to Brad's client. Do I direct my comments to Brad or directly to the Seller?"

"What do you think would be the best way of communicating the information to the ultimate decision maker?"

"Well, it would make sense to speak directly to the Seller, but I don't want to upset Brad in the process," I replied.

"Alan, you need to remember who your client is," Ryan reminded me. "The only person you need to concern yourself with is Greg. No one else's feelings matter. You are his agent, and so you need to think of yourself as though you were Greg's lawyer. Whatever is best for Greg is what you need to be about."

"But what about maintaining relationships with the other agents? I don't want to burn any bridges with Brad. He's pretty successful, and I'm told he knows how to hold a grudge!"

"Certainly you need to be respectful of Brad's relationship with his client, and I would never encourage you to burn any bridges," he conceded, "but I've always believed that our 'salesmanship' comes into play not when we're working with our clients, but when we are working FOR our clients."

"What do you mean?" I asked.

"You and I are licensed by the Real Estate Council as Salespeople, and it's a license I am proud to hold. When we are representing sellers, of course they expect us to use our 'salesmanship' to sell their properties. But when we're representing buyers, I've always believed myself more of a consultant than a salesman. I've never tried to 'sell' a buyer into a property. But when it comes time to negotiate on their behalf, I need to do everything in my power to 'sell' their offer. Does that make sense?"

"100%." I said, a little pumped up by the idea. "So when do I send the offer over for them to review? As soon as they pick up the phone?"

"You'll find that whether you are sitting in a room with the seller or at the end of a phone line, there is only one thing they will be interested in hearing, and that's the price. I believe that as soon as you offer up that piece of information, their brain switches from 'consideration mode' and goes into 'counter mode.' They start to think of their response to the price, rather than accepting any further information to consider."

"But do you think a sophisticated seller is going to budge from their bottom line price just because we explain all the things that are wrong with his property?" I ask. "I was always told to head into a negotiation with a "walk away number" to avoid slipping too low.

"Who said anything about getting the seller to drop below his bottom line price?" asked Ryan. "It isn't about beating the seller into submission for our clients, but it is about finding a solution that works for all parties. Has Greg told you that his objective is to steal the property? Or even buy it below market value?"

"No."

"Price is only one part of the negotiation, but it happens to be the one that concerns the sellers the most. If the seller is stuck on a number, what other concessions can we get to help Greg get the right deal? What other factors are important to him?"

"Well I know he's concerned about the costs of restoring the home, and he'd feel better about moving forward if there was some assurance things wouldn't get out of hand once he gets a better handle on the problems."

"Good. What else?"

I looked down at my cup of coffee, trying to think of other aspects of this deal that could be better for Greg. "He really would prefer to get into the house earlier than we've got on the offer, but the eviction notice will give them almost 90 days to move out."

"Perfect!" Ryan says enthusiastically. "There are two great negotiating points for you to bear in mind if you find resistance to Greg's offering price. So let's think about what we know. First, the seller is thinking of tearing down the house if he can't get a deal done soon, so anything above the lot value may be appealing," he said, "but we also know that the current revenue from the tenants has real value to an investor... and to the seller. We also know that the property hasn't attracted an offer in nearly 6 months which has to be frustrating for everybody involved. We know that Greg's objectives are to get into the house as soon as possible to avoid paying a further three months' rent, and that he is concerned with the potential for mounting restoration costs. Finally, we know that the tenants are growing marijuana in the house, and while it may not be on a big scale, it certainly would be grounds for immediate eviction."

"That makes things much more interesting than I suspected they might be when I got up this morning," I smiled. "I guess it's my job to line up all that information in a way that allows us to find a solution that everybody can live with."

The Call

The clock on the wall read 8:40 and I picked up the phone to call Brad, anxious to make sure the three-way calling feature works.

"Alan, I've got a 9:00 appointment that I've got to get to," says Ryan. "Good luck with your call."

"You're leaving?" I say as my eyes widen and my throat constricts. "Can't you stick around in case I need you?"

"You won't need me. Just take it slow and be sure to remember who you are representing here. Your objective is to help Greg buy that house at a price he can afford and with favourable terms," he said, truly confident in my abilities. "Greg called you to help him buy this house... not me."

The door clicked shut behind him and the room seemed very empty. I put the phone back down on the cradle to gather myself and muster up a bit more courage. Another long pull on my coffee, and picked up the handset one more time.

"Good morning Brad, it's Alan Stewart calling."

"Good morning Alan. Glad to hear from you. I spoke with my client last night and he thought your solution was a good one. He's waiting for us to call."

"Great. I thought it would be good to just be sure we are on the same page before we call him. The last thing I want to do is offend you or overstep any boundaries."

"Like what?"

"If it's alright with you, I'd like to speak freely and directly with your client Brad, and when I'm done, I'll send you both the offer and excuse myself from the conversation," I continued. "If there is anything you think is offside discussing with him, I'd appreciate it if you could let me know now."

"Mr. Steves is a pretty sophisticated seller Alan, so I'm not too concerned about what you'd like to tell him about your client or your offer. The only thing I'd ask is that you understand that the tenants are the children of close friends of Mr. Steves and I haven't brought up the matter of the plants your contractor found in the crawl space."

"That puts me in a pretty uncomfortable position Brad." I swallowed. "Can you please advise him as soon as we get him on the line? I don't mind if you tell him that I just brought it up, but it's important he understands some of the concerns of my buyer."

While I knew that Ryan would likely disapprove of the fact that I was encouraging Brad to lie to the Seller, I wanted Brad to know that I was on his side. The facts were the facts, and I saw little reason to add more tension to the conversation by not helping Brad hide the fact that he hadn't been completely forthcoming to his client.

"I guess there's no way to avoid it," conceded Brad. "Sure, I'll let him know, then I'll turn the call over to you."

"Thanks. If you can give me his number I'll dial him into the conversation."

I wrote down the number, asked Brad to hang on, and clicked the hang-up switch on the phone. When I heard the dial tone I dialed the number and as soon as the line started ringing I clicked the switch one more time and was reconnected to Brad.

"Hello?" said the third voice on the line.

"Good morning Mr. Steves. It's Brad here and I have Alan Stewart on the line."

"Thanks for calling. I hear you have an offer for me?" said Mr. Steves expectantly.

"I do, Sir. Thanks for taking our call this morning. Before we get started, I would like Brad to explain something to you that we've uncovered through our preliminary inspection."

"Mr. Steves," chimed in Brad. "It turns out that the tenants had four marijuana plants in the crawl space. While we don't suspect that we're dealing with a significant grow-op, there was a locked room we haven't been able to gain access to and so Alan's client is concerned about what might be going on in there."

"And rightly so," Mr. Steves added. "That's really disappointing Brad. I thought you were checking in on the place?"

Trying to deflect some of the blame and the negativity forming around this information, I cut in, "Mr. Steves, it's Alan here. My sense of it is that the tenants simply stashed the plants in the crawlspace during our visit. For all we know, they may well have just moved them there from outside to hide them, however, until we are able to access that room we are moving forward with the assumption that there is no problem. I only wanted you to know that if there is evidence that if the house has been used for growing marijuana, we will have to re-open the negotiations as it will have a negative impact on the value of the property."

"That's fair enough." injected Mr. Steves.

"Mr. Steves, I'm going to let Alan take over here to present his offer to you and explain a few things." Brad advised. "Once he is finished I'll call you back so we can review things. I'd ask that you not make concessions or discuss pricing until you and I have had a chance to speak. Is that reasonable?"

"Yes, of course." said Mr. Steves. "Alan, can you send me the offer now so we can review it point by point?"

"Mr. Steves, I'm going to hold off on sending you the offer for one very simple reason," I responded. "If I were you, the only thing I would be interested in at this point is the price. But my clients offer is reflective of a few significant issues that we need to address. If we can't find a way to address those issues, the price is likely irrelevant."

"Look Alan, I appreciate that you want to hold my attention, but I have a 9:30 appointment, so I'd prefer if we can cut to the chase."

"I understand that Sir. I'll be brief," I promised. "As you know, our contractor found dry-rot issues in the north wall of the building. While we are concerned that they may be structural, there's no way of knowing for sure until we open up the wall. While my client has been pre-approved for financing, he is concerned about the potential cost of repairing structural issue. We've been given an estimate to correct what we can assess at this point, but if the cost goes well in excess of that amount, my client isn't in a position to cover the costs."

"Alan, I'm not selling a new house." retorted Mr. Steves. "We all know that there are going to be costs involved if your client wants to make improvements or renovate."

"Of course, but we are not talking about maintenance issues or improvements in this case. If the issue of dry-rot is significant and affects the structure of the building, it's going to mean a significant change in the value of the home."

"So where to do we go from here then? I'm not prepared to accept an offer that includes an allowance for correcting a deficiency that we don't even know exists," he argued.

"Of course not. But what we would like to do is negotiate a price that reflects a reasonable estimate to correct the issues we're now aware of, assuming they are not structural. But if it becomes evident that the structure is affected, we would ask that you look after the cost of remediation."

"How do you propose we do that?"

"In the offer, we've included what is known as a hold back clause. In essence, we will have the lawyer keep back an amount of the purchase price that would be sufficient to cover the costs in the event that structural elements need to be replaced. This would have to be determined by a structural engineer that you can select, at my client's cost, to prepare a report once the walls and floor has been removed."

"So how long will this all take?" Mr. Steves asked.

"My client is prepared to do the work within 30 days of getting possession of the house."

"I'll give that some thought," he replied.

"I appreciate that. Now, the other significant issue we have to address is the tenants," I continued. "Brad tells me that you have a relationship with the tenants, and as such, we certainly wouldn't want to suggest you evict based on what was found in the crawl space, as would likely be your right."

"No, no. I couldn't do that. The tenants are the children of some of my dearest friends," he explained.

"Given your relationship, perhaps you they would be prepared to vacate earlier so that my client can avoid paying additional rent. In fact, I know of a mobile home on a nice lot in the neighbourhood that I think would be perfect for them. The owner may even rent it to them with an option to buy."

"Let's cross that bridge when we come to it Alan. Until I know what your client is prepared to pay, I'm really not interested in negotiating the terms."

I could sense that his patience was running thin and I was nervous about offending him.

"I understand Mr. Steves so let's get to the offer. I'm going to send it to you now Brad so you can forward it to Mr. Steves. While we're waiting, I'll outline the subjects for you. As I mentioned, my client is pre-qualified for a mortgage of this size, however, the bank requires an appraisal. Secondly, while we have had a contractor go through the property, we are going to have qualified building and septic inspector prepare a report at considerable expense to my client to ensure we know what we are buying. We expect the roof and the hot water tank to be flagged as requiring replacement, but we are not going to renegotiate on those points as my client appreciates that it is an older home and there are going to be ongoing maintenance issues. We have reviewed the title search and the disclosure statement that Brad provided us and we are satisfied with both of those documents which we have incorporated into the contract."

"I still don't have the offer in my inbox Alan," injected Brad. "Have you sent it through?"

I clicked the SEND button. "You should have it now Brad. Try hitting your Send and Receive button." I could hear the "ding" notification through the phone, indicating he had received it.

"Yes, here it is now. I'll forward it on to you now Mr. Steves."

"While we have set the completion and possession dates for the time you will require to give proper notice to the tenants, we have included a clause that states that we will move the dates forward to the earliest possible time if you are successful in negotiating an earlier departure for your tenants. And finally, our offering price is based on the recent comparable sales, which I have included for you at the end of the email, and an adjustment for the amount we expect to spend on the repairs to the dry-rot. Our offer price is

8% below your asking price, which may be less than you were hoping for, but it is significantly more than what you would ever be able to attain for the lot alone. I've shown your house half a dozen times and given the feedback I've received... tearing it down may be your only option if you don't get a deal done here with my buyer."

I could hear another "ding" as the offer made its way to Mr. Steves' inbox. There was a long pause... "I've got the offer here Alan.... Brad and I will discuss it and let you know."

"Thank you for your attention Mr. Steves, and thank you for the opportunity Brad," I concluded. "The offer is open until 6:00pm this evening." I almost said that my client is able to "respond" any time after 3:30pm, but caught myself by realizing that this would signal Greg's willingness to entertain a counter offer.

"Alan," Mr. Steeves added, "is this your client's best offer?"

I paused, thinking through my response. "We feel that our offer accurately reflects the value of the property given all the factors we've discussed and I'm confident you will come to the same conclusion."

"Okay, thanks Alan," said Brad. "We will be in touch."

I hung up the phone and fell back into my chair. I felt 10 feet tall, knowing that I had done all I could to put Greg's offer in the best light. I may have crossed the line with Brad a little with my suggestion to his client that the house may not be worth anything to anyone else, but I wanted to be sure Mr. Steves knew that we understood his other option, and therefore the value that our offer presented.

Ryan had told me to never forget that while doing the deal was exciting for us as agents, it was more often an emotional roller coaster for our clients. As such, I leaned back into the phone and dialed Greg's cell phone.

"Greg? It's Alan."

"Oh hey Alan, I thought you'd never call! What's happening?"

"Well, the seller and his agent and I had a lengthy conversation on the phone this morning and I did everything I could to promote your offer in his eyes. I'd be surprised if we didn't get a response from him Greg, but it's too early to say what it will be. He has until 6:00 tonight to respond, and all I can tell you is that he had a 9:30am appointment, so I'd be surprised if we hear back from him straight away."

"All right," he said, a little disappointed that I didn't have more information. "I'll have my cell phone with me throughout the day, so call me as soon as you know something."

"You bet. Hang in there Greg."

We hung up the phone and I suddenly felt the pressure to get a deal done for Greg. It was obvious to me that he was still committed to the house, and that he'd be disappointed if he didn't get it.

Negotiating for Buyers

I carried on with my day, not expecting to hear from Brad or Mr. Steves until closer to 6:00pm, but it was only a little after 10:00 when Kim called over to me to let me know that Brad was on Line 2.

"Hi Brad. How did we make out?" I asked.

"Pretty well, Alan," Brad said, sounding surprised. "I think that Mr. Steves was expecting a real stink bid after you described all the work that might need to be done, and the offer price actually fell in line with his expectations."

"Well that's good news." I replied. "How did he feel about the terms and conditions?"

"He's fine with the dates, and he tells me that he'll have the tenants contact you about that place you mentioned. Between you and me, I think he put the screws to them a little over the marijuana plants, and as such, they'll probably be more cooperative."

"I know my client would appreciate that and I'm sure Mr. Steves would be pleased to have his money sooner rather than later."

"You're right. But the holdback amount is a different matter. Mr. Steves feels that the worst case scenario wouldn't be any more than $10,000 and he feels that a $20,000 holdback is effectively holding him ransom."

"I know it's a lot of money on a deal of this size, but does he understand that he'll get back anything that's left over?"

"He does, but he's not prepared to have any more than $10,000 held back from the deal. Other than that, everything is acceptable." Brad said. "See what you can do with your guy. We're still open until 6:00 pm."

"OK, send through the contract and I'll get it to my buyer for a response."

"No problem. Mr. Steves is having his secretary scan it to us both."

It was all I could do not to phone Greg with the information Brad had given to me, but it turned out to be a good thing I didn't. Ryan had a policy of never negotiating on a deal until it was in writing. It was often frustrating for other agents and clients, but he knew that it was a critical element of maintaining his reputation as a professional. Within 15 minutes the contract showed up in my inbox.

I opened the email and reviewed the changes that Mr. Steves had made on the screen. On page one of the contract, rather than accept our price, Mr. Steves had stricken out our offer and increased the purchase price amount by $5000. I was surprised given the fact that Brad had just told me he had accepted the price. Everything else looked in order.

I called Brad back and asked for an explanation.

"You're kidding!" said Brad. "He told me he was fine with the price. Sorry about that Alan... I guess he changed his mind."

I finished up with Brad, telling him how thankful I was for not having communicated his verbal counter offer to my client, which may have had a significant bearing on the good will of the negotiations. I then turned my attention to Greg.

"Hi Greg, its Alan. Can you come over at lunch to review the counter offer? It's just been sent over to me."

"Can't you just tell me how he's responded? Did he accept our offer?" Greg pleaded.

"Greg, there's a lot to review," I said. "While the other agent led me to believe he might, he hasn't accepted our price. He has come back with a $5000 increase and I think you should be pleased with that. But he's made some other changes that we should discuss in person. We still have until 6:00 tonight to respond."

"Okay, I'll see you at 12:15."

When Greg showed up, he looked excited. His energy level was high, and I was pretty sure that we were going to get a deal done. Kim offered Greg a coffee or a cup of tea, but he refused both, obviously anxious to get down to business. I grabbed Greg's file from the "Offers in Process" tray and we sat down together at the meeting table.

"Alright Greg, here it is," I said as I extracted the scanned and printed pages, complete with Mr. Steves initials and signatures. "As I mentioned, I think the price is really fair... but he's not prepared to protect you to the same extent as we wanted with the holdback amount."

"That's not good. How much will he put aside?"

"It's here on page 5. He's changed it from $20,000 to $10,000," I explained. "That means if the costs come in more than that, it'll be on your shoulders. But if there's no structural damage, it's not something we're looking for him to cover anyway."

"And how about the tenants?" he asked. "Anyway to get them out sooner?"

"That's another positive. It turns out that the tenants have a relationship with the owner and he's agreed to have me show them a rental property that I think might be good for them."

"Oh ya? Which property is that?"

"Yours," I replied with a wink. Greg's current rental was a nice little mobile home on a big lot close to the village. He told me that his landlord had offered to sell it to him when he started looking for houses to purchase, but Greg didn't like the idea of owning a mobile. "It seemed like a reasonable solution."

"Oh you're clever," he replied. "Well, given all that, where do I sign?"

"You need to initial this price change... and this change in the holdback... and that's it." I said with a smile, extending my hand to him. "Congratulations! You've got a deal."

I photocopied the contract and gave Greg a copy and gave him a list of all the home inspectors and septic inspectors in our neighbourhood.

"Your homework is to decide on a couple of inspectors and to get this copy of your contract over to your banker so they can make arrangements for the appraisal," I advised him. "I'd recommend you be present for the inspections, and don't forget to confirm that your folks will be available for whatever day you work out. We should give the tenants as much notice as possible, and certainly no less than 24 hours' notice. Just let me know what date you work out and I'll have Brad make the arrangements."

"Thanks Alan," he said sincerely. "I know you're surprised I'm buying this place after all that's happened, but you've done a really good job in making me feel like I'm protected. Please pass on my thanks to Ryan as well."

I was looking forward to telling Ryan all about the day's events more than Greg could know. I found myself really wanting to do a good job for him, to protect his reputation by doing things the way I knew he would. It was a challenge that I knew would only do good things for me in the long run.

When Ryan came through the door in time for coffee at 2:00 that afternoon, I had left him a copy of the deal, rolled into a tube and tied in a neat red ribbon.

"What's this?" he inquired.

I didn't turn to look at him, rather, I stared into the computer screen.

"You'll have to read it," Kim said to him, teasingly.

I could hear the paper unroll and then unexpectedly, he roared out with a loud "Whaa-hooo!!" followed by four loud clangs of the brass bell. I turned and saw the look of sincere pleasure on his face as he walked towards me with his hand outstretched for a congratulatory handshake. "Well done my boy! Well done."

Greg removed all his subjects and completed on the purchase. He spent the next year doing a lot of the work that Tom recommended himself, and wound up selling the property three years later for a decent profit, calling me to list and sell it. And the tenants remembered my helpfulness and wound up asking me to help them buy Greg's rental mobile home... with the help of their parents.

What seemed like a small deal starting out turned into four transactions: the original sale, the mobile owner's exclusive listing, the tenants' purchase and finally Greg's sale of his renovated house.

CHAPTER 5

WORKING WITH SELLERS

In my role as a Buyer's Agent, I relied almost exclusively on leads that were generated through Ryan's listings, whether in hosting open houses or responding to inquiries on the phone or email. But we agreed that if I were able to secure any listings for the team, I would receive 50% of the commission from the sale, even though Ryan would be responsible for the costs associated with it. The only caveat was that if the clients I secured to list were already in Ryan's data base of approximately 1500 people, I would only receive 25%. Because of the difference in our age and the people we associated with, I didn't expect any conflicts.

I expected that people would be looking for my help in listing their homes as soon as I got my license. Given my contacts in the community through my volunteer work, affiliation and status as a founding member of our local Rotary Club, my business contacts and all the friends we had made through the local schools, how long would it take to get a listing?

But people seemed to ignore that fact that I was able to help them. For some reason, people who I felt very close to refused to call me when they needed help selling their homes. Not being one to shy away from getting to the bottom of things, I asked a soccer team mate of mine why they listed their house with the competition.

"Hey Barry," I said as we took a water break. "I see you listed your house with Daryl Phillips. Do you mind if I ask why you didn't give me a call?"

"Oh hey Al," Barry responded. "I felt bad about that, but Daryl sold me that house, and I just felt really uncomfortable about not listing it with him. Daryl actually loaned us some of the down payment we needed when we bought it. I hope you can understand."

"No problem Barry," I said. "Daryl is a great guy, and I'm sure he'll do a good job for you. I'll do whatever I can to help bring a buyer for you."

And so it went. After a half dozen or so disappointments, I wondered if even my mother would list her house with me!

It wasn't long after that, as I sat in my hairdresser's chair, that I had an epiphany. As I commiserated with my hairdresser, I realized that people were, in general, loyal to their Realtors® just the same way as they are loyal to their hairdressers. While hair stylists built meaningful relationships with people through regular, close, physical contact and intimate conversations, Realtors® build relationships with people by caring for them as they endured one of the largest, most emotional and stressful transactions of their lives.

And then it happened. I was in the office one morning when the phone rang.

"Good morning Alan. It's Joan Christian calling. Fred and I have been thinking about finding a bigger place and we wondered if you could help us?"

Joan and Fred were clients of mine from the cabinet shop and we had really hit it off when I did a little renovation project for her recreational property the year before. Joan and her sister Christy came by the shop every time they were in town and I'd like to think that we were friends.

"Of course Joan," I replied excitedly. "Are you at the cottage now? I'm free this afternoon if you'd like me to come by to prepare an evaluation?"

"That would be great Alan. Why don't you come over around 3:00? I'll have the coffee on."

"Perfect. Joan, do you mind if I bring my partner along? He's got lots of experience and I'd appreciate his input."

"Of course not. We'll see you at 3:00."

I could hardly contain myself. "Kim! I just got a listing appointment! My first one."

"That's great Alan" she dutifully responded. "You'll be great."

I called Ryan on his cell phone and asked him if he could join me that afternoon.

"I wouldn't miss it Alan." he said. "I'm going to have to shuffle things around a bit, but give me the address and I'll see you there."

Preparing for the Listing Appointment

I finished up the property search I was working on for an internet client, sent him the results, and spent the rest of the day trying to find out everything I could about Joan's property. I pulled up the old listing data sheet, the tax assessment, and the lot plan and put them into a Blue Folder and asked Kim to prepare a label with the address and client's name on it. I called the municipality's planning office and asked if there were anything I should know about in their file that may affect the value of the property.

"I'm sorry but we can't give out that information on the phone. You'll need to come and see us at the Planning Department if you'd like to review the file with a planner."

It was a 1 / 2 hour drive to the municipal offices, but I knew exactly what Ryan would tell me if asked: "*Alan*," he'd say. "*These folks are prepared to pay you tens of thousands of dollars to sell their house for them... what do you think you should do?*"

"I'll be there in half an hour," I told the voice at the other end of the phone.

With the blue file folder stowed safely in my briefcase, I headed out the door and into my car where I reviewed my checklist before pulling out.

Listing Checklist / Information Sheet

Listing Date			Expiry Date	
Name (1)		☐Primary	Cell	☐Text OK
email			Other	
Name (2)		☐Primary	Cell	☐Text OK
email			Other	
Property Address				
Mailing Address				
Showings				
Notes				

Compile Prior to Listing Appointment ☑

Clipboard and 2 pens	Digital Camera Kit
Tablet / Laptop	Tripod
Sample marketing material presentation	Additional memory card
Business Cards	Additional battery - charged
Agency Brochure	Tape and Bosch DLR130K Laser Measure
Pre-Printed Listing Agreement	Yard Sign with inserts
Property Condition Disclosure	Mallet and tool kit with knife and zap straps
FINTRAC ID Forms	Lock Box
CMA	Spray Paint and spray can trigger
MLS Data Input Forms	Work Gloves

To Do List During and After Listing Appointment ☑

Agency Brochure, PCDS, FINTRAC & Listing Agreement Completed	Prepare Ad Copy ⊔ Client's Approved
Copy of Documents to Seller or Access to Online Folder	Prepare Feature Sheet w/ floor plan ⊔ Client's Approved
Home Measurements and Floor Plan Ordered	Listing Package Provided to Office
Photos Ordered / Taken	For Sale Sign Installed ⊔ Custom Rider
Obtain Keys / Lockbox Code or Key #	Arrange Date for Agents Open:
Complete Data Input Sheet	Arrange Date for Public Open:
Taxes and Title Confirmed / Charges Ordered	Order Just Listed Postcards and distribute
Obtain Strata Plan / Lot Plan	Contact REALTORS with nearby listings
Obtain Financials and Bylaws (Strata)	Review MLS Input for any errors
Listing on Sales Board in Office	Launch Social Media Campaign

Upon Accepted Offer / Upon Firm Sale

Upon Accepted Offer	Upon Firm Sale
Transaction Record Sheet to Office	Subject Removal to Office
Contract and Deposit to Office	Buyer's Lawyer:
Deposit increase date:	Seller's Lawyer:
Mortgage Approved By:	Referral Form (if applicable)
Strata Docs by date:	Install SOLD sign
Inspections by date:	Order Change of Address Cards for Sellers
Other Subjects by date:	Order Just Sold Postcards and distribute

Immediately Prior to Closing

Remove Sign	Call Clients to ensure document signing completed
Purchase closing gift	Arrange for keys to buyers and possession instructions
Meet Buyers and Agent on Possession Date	Deliver Client Gift 2 days after possession

"Listing file? Check. Camera? Check. Extra battery and memory card? Check. Tape measure? Check. Clipboard? Check. Graph Paper? Check. Blank listing agreement? Check. Pen? Check...."

(See Appendix E: Pre-Listing Appointment Checklist)

I pulled into the parking lot of the Regional District and grabbed a couple of business cards from my glove box. At the front desk I asked to see someone from the Planning Department they asked me to take a seat while they called someone to come to meet me at the information desk.

"Can I help you?" asked a young man about my age with glasses and a "Miami Vice" stubble.

"I hope so," I replied. "My name is Alan Stewart and I'm a Realtor® preparing an evaluation on a house. I called in a little while ago and the gal told me that I would have to come down to have a look at your file to see if there were anything in it that might affect its value."

"OK. Do you have a letter of authority from the homeowner for you to act as her agent?" he asked.

"No. The person I spoke with didn't say anything about that and I just drove 35 kilometers to get here," I said, apologetically and fearing the worst.

"That's OK," he said. "I won't be able to give you copies of the documents in the file without it, but we can still help you gather information about the property. To be honest, I wish more Realtors® would do this kind of research before listing a house so that we wouldn't have to clean up messes afterwards."

"Does that happen often?" I asked.

"Oh you'd be surprised! Sometimes I think the listing Realtors® just don't want to know about problems for fear of making it harder to sell a place. But there is nothing worse than having to break bad news to someone during their negotiations, or God forbid, after they've removed their subjects."

"Really? That happens?"

"I probably have to deal with one or two files a month with new property owners pleading to make changes to zoning or restrictions because they didn't get all the facts up front."

"Ouch!   I wouldn't want to be one of their Realtors®" I said laughingly.

"Nope," he returned. "I'm guessing they don't see a lot of repeat clients!"

The hairdresser analogy came back to mind. Certainly one way to lose the loyalty of a customer would be to give them a really bad haircut. For Realtors®, I guessed that bad advice, or lack of information, would likely have the same impact.

"Well, I'm going to do my best to do it right and I certainly appreciate any advice you may have for me."

"It would be a pleasure," he said, passing me his business card. "My name is Scott. You can call me anytime."

We spent about 10 minutes reviewing the file which included a number of plans, building permits, occupancy permits and an easement in favour of the Regional District that allowed them, or the neighbouring highland properties, to clean out a culvert on the property for drainage.

"Looks pretty clean, all-in-all" Scott said. And then with a wink and an outstretched hand he finished up. "Good luck with getting the listing"

On the drive back to the office I started thinking about how I wanted the meeting to go and how I wanted to make sure that Joan felt confident in my ability to do a good job. I started scripting how things were going to go in my head:

"Joan, I want you to know that while I am new to the role of being a Realtor®, I'm not new to Real Estate, sales and marketing or the world of business." *Oh, that sounds good. Now to back it up.*

"Before moving here and pursuing my dream of operating the cabinet shop, I was employed as the Vice President of Sales and Marketing of a significant transportation company in Vancouver, and I was responsible for dealing with numerous clients in countries around the Pacific Rim which helped me hone my negotiating skills. Before that I spent 3 years as a Sales Representative for a multinational office equipment company, being taught everything I would ever need to know about sales and marketing in the trenches."

But what about my lack of experience in selling real estate specifically? "Joan, I've always prided myself in being aligned with the right people, particularly in business, and that is why I chose to work alongside someone who has a great deal of experience and a track record of success to ensure that our team will give your home the very best chance of selling for the most money in the shortest time possible."

And a little more support? "There is one other thing I want you to know about to help reassure you that you are making the right decision Joan. Our office is the top selling office in our market area and the company's commitment to maintaining exceptional professional standards and cooperation amongst our sales people is unmatched. When you hire me, you are getting all the benefits of working with our team PLUS the strengths of our entire company. How does that sound?"

"It sounds frickin' great!" I thought to myself. I rehearsed the speech a few more times which, combined with all the research I had done, gave me the confidence I needed to walk through the door at Joan's house as a professional Realtor®, not the cabinet maker she knew me as in the past.

I returned to the office and spent the rest of my day looking for any more information I could gather on the property, paying particular attention to what Joan and her family had paid for the property 6 years before, and comparing that to the increase in average and median home prices since then. Having been in the home and having a pretty good recollection of it, I started to build an idea of what it was worth in my mind.

At 2:45 I packed up my file into my briefcase and headed to my car.

"Wish me luck Kim!" I said as I grabbed the door handle.

"What for? You probably know more about that property than your client and Ryan combined!" she laughed. "Don't sweat it... you're going to get it!"

"I didn't know you were a poet Kim," I said. "Do you mind if I write that one down?"

I never asked Kim if she came up with that little ditty on her own, but it stuck with me for the next year, every time I was preparing to head into a listing appointment. *"Don't sweat it... you're going to get it! Don't sweat it... you're going to get it! Don't sweat it... you're going to get it."*

I'm convinced that this mantra, along with the confidence I built by doing my homework before ever going to a listing appointment, were often the determining factor in securing as many listings as I did. I used to laugh about it with my wife. I'd say, "People are like dogs... They can SMELL fear." And the last thing that someone selling their house wanted in a Realtor® was someone who wasn't absolutely confident in their ability.

"Don't sweat it... You're going to get it!" I said out loud one more time as I got out of the car at Joan's place at 2:55.

The Initial Meeting

"Alan," Joan called out through the screen door. "You're early! Come on in."

"Hi Joan," I said as I pulled open the screen door, the springs and hinges squeaking and reminding me of my family's cabin... and settling me down a notch. "How are you?" I said as I bent down to pet Joan's old Jack Russell terrier who had made his way over to see who had stopped by.

"I'm great thanks!" she said with a smile on her face. "I'm just mixing up some lemonade for us. Is your partner coming?"

"You bet. He had an earlier appointment so he told me he would meet us here at 3 o'clock. In fact, I think I hear him now," I responded.

"Well please show him around," she said. I'll meet you out front in a minute."

"Sure thing," I agreed. "Do you mind if I leave my bags inside?"

"Just set them on the table."

I did as she asked, grabbed my camera, and headed out to meet Ryan who was putting his keys in the pocket of his pants. "Right on time," I called out.

"What a beautiful spot this is," Ryan said, loud enough for Joan to hear. "You know, I've driven past this driveway a million times, but never knew how charming the property was once you were off the road. It's delightful."

"Well Joan has asked that I show you around a bit while she gets some drinks ready for us. Where would you like to start?" I asked.

"Let's start where every buyer will want to start."

"Where's that?" I asked.

"At the waterfront!" he said. "Whenever you visit a property for the first time, always try and put yourselves in the mind of a prospective purchaser. You need to figure out the 'story' of the property."

"Story?" I asked again.

"Sure. Every home has a story or two. Of course there is the story of its past and all the memories that were made there, but our job is to really understand the story of its future," he said. "A property like this is about a lot more than concrete and studs. It's about memories of swimming off the dock and bringing home salmon for dinner."

We walked along the side of the house and as we got to the bottom of the stairs I started to get a sense of this property's 'story.' Two kayaks hung neatly under the sundeck and the walls by the back door were lined with paddles, fishing rods, nets and lifejackets. The grass had been recently cut and edged, but the natural vegetation led me to believe that spending time working in the yard was not priority one around here.

I stopped to take a couple photos along the way to the water's edge, appreciating what it must feel like to live here. "It's pretty cool," I said to Ryan.

"It really is," he replied. "Do you think the value of the property is in the 2x4's and materials used in building the cottage or the land that it's sitting on?"

"It's a combination of the two really. The cottage isn't all that special and it needs some work, but it's really charming and it kind of makes sense for this property."

"That's the story, and that's the art behind developing a good sense of the market value." Ryan said, seemingly excited that I recognized that the cottage, while of little value as a building unto itself, actually added significant value to the property because it was appropriate and charming.

Ryan was ALWAYS positive about people's properties. He confided in me that he made a habit of looking for all the positives in a property and trying not to focus on any of the negatives during the first meeting. As we walked to the water's edge and clearly out of earshot of Joan, Ryan expanded on the idea: "Alan, a property is worth more to the homeowner than to anyone else. Just like when we look in the mirror, our brains tend to ignore all our little bumps and imperfections. A buyer, on the other hand, has to see past all the bumps and imperfections which jump out at THEM like a sore thumb."

"But don't you need to factor 'the bumps and imperfections' into your evaluation?"

"Yes of course. But today isn't the day for that conversation. Take notes about the issues, but today we want to celebrate the property with the homeowner. This is a very emotional time for them, and we want to be sure that they know we are on their side."

"Sure, but doesn't that set their expectations too high?"

"All I know is that we can't help people like Joan unless they hire us to work for them," he returned. "If our job is to help our clients, our first responsibility is to get the job. If you had a valuable painting that you needed to sell at auction, who would you hire to sell it? Someone who believed in the artist and appreciated every aspect of the painting, or someone who spent all his time picking it apart? Who do you think would be able to help you reach your objectives of selling that painting for the best possible return?"

"Fair enough. I'll have to remember to add "rose coloured glasses" to my checklist of things to bring to a listing appointment," I said, earning a chuckle out of Ryan.

It wasn't long before Joan called us up to the deck overlooking the shore to enjoy a glass of lemonade and cookies. After a brief introduction and some interesting discussions about Joan and Fred's adventures in their kayaks, I asked Ryan to give us his impressions of the property.

"Well Joan, not even having a look through the home yet, I can tell you that your property is very desirable in this market and I really love the fact that you have left so much of the natural landscaping. One thing that buyers look for in recreational properties is low maintenance landscaping, so that's a real plus."

"I'm glad to hear that Ryan," said Joan, who looked very interested in Ryan's opinions. "I was concerned that we hadn't done enough in the yard to get it ready for sale."

"No, it's perfect," Ryan continued. "It's obvious how much you love the property in the care you take of it. I can only imagine all the wonderful memories you and your family must have shared here." He paused. "Our job in marketing the property is to have potential buyers understand that we're selling more than just a building on a lot; we need to communicate all the benefits associated with owning it... like strengthening family bonds while sharing time together in the kayaks, making friends by enjoying lemonade in the Summer sun on the deck, just like this, and making lifelong memories while fishing with the grandkids from the shoreline. Does that make sense?"

"Perfect sense Ryan." Joan said as she sank back into her deck chair. "I was so concerned you were going to tell me the cottage was a tear down! I'm really pleased to hear that you see just how special our place is."

I saw now exactly why Ryan was so concerned with seeing the positives in a home. When a Realtor® comes to help sellers with an evaluation, property owners feel like they are being judged personally. It's a very emotional time where owners' nerves are exposed until they gain some sense of confidence that their property has somehow made the grade.

"What Alan and I will do today Joan is take some time to gain a better understanding of your home and property and hopefully spend some time with you reviewing that information along with the information we have already gathered to help us all get a better sense of what the current market value of the home may be. Does that meet with your expectations?" asked Ryan.

"Very much. My husband should be home in an hour or so," she said, looking a little concerned. "Is that going to work into your schedule?"

"That will be just fine Joan," I added. "It will take us a fair amount of time to measure the house and do our other due diligence, and it's a perfect day for photos so we'll get started on that aspect of the marketing plan as well if that's OK?"

"Well I'm not sure if the house is ready for photos, but it certainly would be a good day to get photos of the yard."

We thanked Joan for the lemonade and cookies and invited her to join us for the tour of the house. I took the tray of empty glasses and half full pitcher of lemonade and returned it to the kitchen off the deck.

"Okay Joan," Ryan said. "Why don't you show us through your home as though I were an old friend that you wanted to impress? Tell me about all the wonderful things you've done to it, and the little things we may not notice that make it special for you."

"Where should we start?" she asked.

"Well the kitchen is the heart of the home, so let's start and finish right here."

Joan, obviously feeling a little uncomfortable playing tour guide, pointed out the appliance they had installed two years ago and explained that while they intended to replace the linoleum floors, they just never got around to it.

"Should we tile the floors before we put the house on the market?" she asked, directing her question to Ryan.

He rubbed his chin, looking at the condition of the existing flooring. "You know what Joan, I would replace it with a tile or maybe even a slate floor. Alan, can you make a note of that?"

I returned to my bag and took out the notepad and pen and started making a list that I titled "Preparing Home for Sale". As we made our way throughout the home, anytime Joan asked Ryan whether or not she should do something to improve the place he would stop, rub his chin, nod his head while pushing out his lower lip slightly and simply say "I think I would," and I would add it to the list.

The more ideas Ryan accepted as good ones, the more excited Joan got about telling him her plans. It was obvious that she was buying in as part of the team.

As we were led into Joan and Fred's bedroom, Joan turned to us, walking almost backwards into the room and really getting into her role as tour guide. "And this is my very favorite part of the house!"

While the bedroom was a standard rectangular bedroom, and not overly large or ornate, Joan had obviously taken great pride in decorating the bedroom like something from a photo from a cottage magazine. A white linen duvet and lace pillows on a driftwood bed frame surrounded with sea foam blue walls, starfish accents, white flowers overfilling a small glass flower dish and bright white furniture pieces throughout. "And Alan made these beautiful furniture pieces for us Ryan, and I just love them! The whole room makes me feel like I'm in a movie."

"I love how it all came together Joan," I said, not having seen the finished room. "Really amazing."

"Wait until you see the bathroom!"

We carried on through the room, with Joan not offering any "To Do" items to the list. "And that's pretty much it!" said Joan. "What do you think?"

"I love it." said Ryan. "I'm really impressed with what you've done with the house Joan. And while we all appreciate that the building is an older cabin, your personal touches, paint colours, and artwork all add character to virtually every room. You should be proud of it."

"We are... which is why it's going to be so hard to sell," she replied. "But the kids' families are growing and we know that if we're going to continue coming up, we need to find something a little bigger."

"Well I know a really good Realtor® that I'm sure can help you find the perfect home," Ryan said, looking at me and giving Joan a wink, "but for now, we'll focus on helping you get this one sold."

I couldn't help think through the entire experience that Ryan had every expectation of getting the listing. *"Don't sweat it. You're going to get it...."* I wondered whether Ryan had a similar mantra to give him such confidence. Throughout the entire meeting with Joan he included her as part of our team, and after an hour with her, I'm convinced that she felt it as a result of her ideas and input not only being sought and valued and incorporated into how we would market the property for sale.

Ryan and I had finished measuring each room of the house, as well as the outside to determine the square footage and I had set up my tripod and camera with 10mm lens to capture high quality photographs of the interior.

Taking his notes and two other forms out of his binder, Ryan turned to Joan. "Joan, while the house looks terrific, we agree there are a few things that should be taken care of before getting it on the market. I'd like to leave you this list and a handy checklist of all the things a Seller should think about when listing their home for sale." He passed her the paper and added, "I've tried to indicate the kind of return you get on each item by noting 1, 2 or 3 dollar signs. The more dollar signs, the more it's worth considering."

"That's helpful Ryan." said Joan. "I'll go through it with Fred when he gets home."

Seller's Pre-Listing Checklist

Put on a fresh pair of glasses and try and look at your house from a potential buyer's perspective, working from the curb, through the home and into the backyard. Imagine that you were looking to purchase a home like yours. How would your home stack up on the following? Every job on this list will add cash and result in a faster sale. While we shouldn't judge a book by its cover, we all do! Appeal to the Buyer's emotions and you'll come out the winner.

ENTRYWAY	Return	Done	To do	N/A
Check your front door to see if it needs painting.	$$			
Polish door fixtures if needed.	$			
Purchase a fresh welcome mat.	$$			
PAINT		Done	To do	N/A
Paint the outside of your home if needed.	$$			
Paint trim and mouldings if needed	$$$			
LANDSCAPING		Done	To do	N/A
Potted plants and flowers make your home look beautiful and tell a buyer you care	$$$			
Make sure the lawn is cut, weeds are pulled and ground covers look fresh	$$			

DECLUTTER: SHORT TERM PAIN FOR LONG TERM GAIN		Done	To do	N/A
One of the best and least expensive ways to improve the appearance and feel in your home is to clear out your closets and rooms as much as possible. Consider renting a storage locker.	$$$			
A place for everything and everything in its place. If it can't be neatly placed in a drawer or put away on a shelf, box it up.	$$$			
Organize all closets. Make sure it doesn't look like they are overflowing	$$			
Organize and clean out all cabinets and drawers.	$			
Clear all clutter from the countertops. Less is more!	$$			
Remove papers and unnecessary items.	$$			
Organize, straighten and coordinate your hanging space.	$$			

KITCHENS: YOUR HOME'S FOCAL POINT		Done	To do	N/A
Store infrequently used appliances.	$$			
Remove as much as possible from the counters.	$$			
Remove all the fridge magnets and miscellaneous hanging items	$$			
Closets and storage areas:				
Improve perception of size by removing items you aren't using.	$$$			

		Done	To do	N/A
Clean your stove inside and out.	$$$			
Clean the kitchen exhaust hood.	$$$			
Make sure your refrigerator is clean and organized.	$$$			
Clean your counters every day so they look and smell good.	$$$			
Organize the insides of your cabinets; show how much space you have.	$$			
Fresh flowers make a BIG difference for showings.	$$$			
GARAGE: THE MAN CAVE		Done	To do	N/A
Rent a storage locker for excess tools and storage.	$$$			
Consider using concrete paint to cover oil stains if necessary	$$			
GENERAL CLEANING: A SIGN OF CARE.		Done	To do	N/A
Deep Clean. Hire a cleaning service or do it yourself.	$$$			
Surface Clean for freshness before every showings.	$$$			
Have your windows cleaned, inside and out.	$$			
Dust everywhere. It's amazing how much dust you find after you move out.	$$			
FLOORING		Done	To do	N/A

Refinish if necessary or clean and polish all floors.	$$			
Steam clean carpets or replace if necessary, especially if odor is an issue.	$$			
Wash all baseboards	$			

BATHROOMS: A MAKE OR BREAK POINT		Done	To do	N/A
Clean soap residue in a shower.	$$			
Purchase a new shower curtain if it is dirty.	$$$			
Clean accumulated dirt in the track of a sliding shower door.	$$			
Fix soiled or missing grout and apply silicone sealer.	$$			
Clean toilets and tighten lids or replace if necessary.	$$$			
Buy a new bath mat if it looks dirty or tired.	$$			

(See Appendix F: Seller's Pre-Listing Checklist)

Showing Value By Sharing What You Know

"Alan!" Fred said, surprising us all as he walked in through the screen door.

I lifted my head from the eyepiece of the camera and turned to see him coming towards me.

"Hi Fred! Long-time no see."

"Too long," he said shaking my hand. "You look great! How is real estate treating you?"

"I'm really enjoying it Fred. Feels like something I was made for," I replied, turning to Ryan. "Fred, I'd like to introduce you to my partner, Ryan, who has taken me under his wing."

"Hi Ryan, nice to meet you," Fred said. "I've seen your signs all over town and I think we even met at the Stephens' Christmas party a couple of years back."

Joan chimed in, "You're right Fred! I knew we had met before Ryan but I could remember where for the life of me."

"Oh yes," replied Ryan looking a little embarrassed and overcompensating just a bit for not remembering. "The Stephens are great people and Shannon is a very good friend of my wife."

The small talk continued longer than I would have liked, but Ryan made a point of connecting equally with Fred and Joan. He understood very well how important it was to have both husband and wife in agreement on who they chose to market the property.

Ten minutes after the initial introduction the small talk dried up and I chimed in, "Joan and Fred, I've done some homework on your property and I'd like to share the results with you. Can we sit down and review what I've found out?"

Ryan had taught me that there was both a science and art in determining a value on a property. All the things that Ryan and I had spoken about when we talked to Joan about the 'story' of a house would come into play in establishing what a property might be worth on the open market. If we were able to find a buyer who was looking to create a life that was filled with the same types of memories and experiences as Joan and Fred, we would find a buyer who was prepared to pay significantly more money than a buyer who was looking for a different kind of experience.

Working with buyers had taught me that a house has to 'speak' to a purchaser. If it does, they'll break the bank to have it. If it doesn't, it could offer all the value in the world and they would never submit an offer for consideration. This is particularly true in the recreational real estate market where buyers simply don't face the same kind of pressures as buyers in the residential market.

Ryan explained to me that residential home transactions are based on a buyer's needs more than their wants. Maslow's hierarchy of needs puts shelter near the top of the list, but nobody ever went homeless because they weren't able to close a deal on a recreational cottage. The interesting thing was, however, that people would sometimes pay well over what the market should bear for a property because the property spoke to them on an emotional level. And our job for Joan and Fred was to balance a number of factors which included building a "scientific evaluation" of the property and then tempering that with a number of subjective issues which included the seller's expectations and needs in purchasing their next property, the size of the prospective buyer pool, and the likelihood of finding a buyer who would pay for the "emotional appeal" of a property.

While Certified Appraisers spend years studying various way of evaluating a property, Realtors® are trained to assist by drawing conclusions from what's known as a Comparative Market Analysis, which attempts to derive a value on a property based on homes that had sold with similar attributes in a similar market, while making adjustments for variations.

"Joan and Fred, before coming today I took the opportunity to order a title search on your home and pay a visit to the Municipality to gather as much information as I could so we don't make any assumptions when trying to help you value your property," I started. "And I'm happy to report that as far as the Regional

District is concerned, there aren't any issues that might affect the property value."

"We certainly didn't expect you to go to all that trouble Alan," Joan offered. "We're just starting to think about upgrading, and we haven't even told the kids."

"It's all a part of my job Joan. If I expect to earn your business, I better be prepared to show how hard I am prepared to work on your behalf," I replied.

Ryan chimed in, "Joan, regardless of whether or not you decide to move forward in listing your house for sale, this is all excellent experience for Alan. But it's also important for us to understand your intentions and motivation so we can help you in pricing your home accordingly."

"Why would our intentions affect the market value of the house?" asked Fred.

"It wouldn't affect the value of the home Fred, but it may well affect what we recommend as an asking price. With prices rising, we may wish to be more aggressive but that comes at the cost of time. There is a direct relationship between price you offer a house of sale and the time to find a buyer."

"We're happy to wait if it means us being able to get more money," Fred said. "Right Honey?"

"Sure. As you know, we love this place and we don't have to sell so we can wait for the right buyer."

"Fair enough," said Ryan, "but there is a flaw in your strategy."

"How so?" asked Fred, clearly moving into the driver's seat in the conversation.

"Well, given that your intention is to buy back into the market at a higher price, waiting for the market to go up actually costs you money," said Ryan, like a professor shedding light to a class of interested students. "You see, if the market value of homes in our community rises by 10 percent, a $250,000 home will increase in value by $25,000. In the same time, a $500,000 house will increase by $50,000. So by waiting, you are actually $25,000 worse off than if you sold quickly and bought back in."

"That actually makes a lot of sense Ryan. Don't you agree Fred?"

Fred nodded. "I guess you have a point there. So what do you think we're worth now?"

I opened my blue file folder and the neatly sorted packet of information, kept together with a black and silver folding paper clip. "You would be amazed what information is available online these days, and it's getting better every day. Not only can we collect the title search on your property and the legal plans that are registered with it, but we can source information on municipal services, past sales information, tax assessment data, satellite images with lot plans overlaid on top of them and even maps showing where your water and sewer connections are."

"That's amazing," said Fred, starting to pour over the sheets I was spreading out in front of them. "Can I go online and get this information?"

"Some of it is available to the general public, but usually in a limited form. Our Real Estate Board and Associations have negotiated agreements with the owners of the data to allow us to use it to better assist our clients," I answered. "And while this data is very important in helping us build an opinion of value of your property, it's the access to the sales history of other homes in the area combined with an ability to interpret and understand that data which allows Realtors® to really help their clients understand how they fit into the market."

"What is there to analyse?" asked Fred, flipping through some more sheets of comparable properties data sheets I handed him. "We could drive by these homes anytime to see how we stack up against them."

"Of course you could," said Ryan. "But Fred, just like your home has so many special features and a very definite character, the other homes we are going to use as comparables are more than just studs and dirt. They all have their own story, and as Realtors®, it's our job to know and understand what makes them special. Alan and I are on tour at least twice a week, looking at virtually every home that is listed in order to get a better understanding of how they fit into the market and whether or not they offer good value to our buyers. In fact, we advertise a list of "Hot Buys" in our monthly newsletter and Alan and I pick that list based on how we see properties stacking up against the competition on the market."

"So what price do you think we would need to list at in order to make your 'Hot Buys' list?" asked Joan.

"Great question Joan," replied Ryan. "But it's a little premature. While I have an idea of the range we are going to have to fall into to affect a sale, we never give an opinion of value without being able to back it up. We'll need a day to digest all the information, scrutinize the best comparable properties from the ones we've gathered, and prepare a report for you to review."

"I am going to leave you a copy of all the information that we've gathered so that we are all working from the same page," I added. "While determining the market value is an important step, what really matters for you is the differential cost of upgrading to a new property. Am I right?"

Fred nodded in agreement with his head still down, flipping through the information I had given him.

"And have you talked to the bank about financing the additional amount?" Ryan asked.

"We haven't gotten into specifics with them," Fred said, "But we met with our banker last week and he's given us the green light in principle. He needed to know how much we were going to need to buy a new place and that's when we called you to help us figure things out."

"Great. Part of your homework is to visit our website where you can easily do a property search of all the houses on the market that would meet your criteria in order to determine how much you are likely going to have to spend to get what you want. Is that OK?"

"No problem," said Joan. "I love looking at houses online and Fred doesn't mind either, do you Fred?"

"Not at all," he said, finally lifting his head from the package of paper. "But shouldn't we be looking at all the properties that are available? Not just the ones on your website?"

"We actually have a search tool on our website that allows you to look at ALL the properties listed on the Multiple Listing Service (MLS), not just the ones our clients have listed," said Ryan, proud of this feature which we had added shortly after my arrival.

"And so long as we can come to terms on how much your property is worth, how much you are going to have to spend on a property that will meet your needs, and the monthly expense for the difference, you should have all the information you need to help you decide if you are ready to list the home on the market."

"That sounds great, Alan," said Fred, standing up in expectation of our departure.

Ryan and I stood and thanked our hosts for their hospitality and their time. I gave Joan a hug, which was our custom, before gathering all my things and heading for the door.

"Thanks again for calling, Joan and Fred," I closed. "Your trust and confidence means a lot to me."

"Our pleasure, Alan," said Joan. "You've already proven yourself through all the hard work you put in today. You really have gone above and beyond our expectations."

As I walked back to the car, I felt like I had just completed a $10,000 job interview... and I knew it went great!" It was then that I realized that I hadn't made my sales pitch. After rehearsing my lines in the car, I had sold Joan and Fred on my value not by reciting a script or overcoming objections. The effort I had put into my preparation and the value I had given them before even listing the property had done all the selling for me.

The Debriefing and Coming To Terms with Value

I arrived back at the office shortly after Ryan, who was sitting in his car on his cell phone. I headed in, excited to tell Kim about our experience.

"How did it go?" asked Kim with a grin as I came through the door.

"Great, I think. It turned out that Joan and Fred had met Ryan before and have a few mutual friends. Thank God he was there! I couldn't believe how many questions they had and how I had to rely on Ryan for so much help. I guess you really don't know what you don't know until you're asked!?"

"Isn't that the truth!?" said Kim as she pointed to her screen, highlighted a block of text and pasted it into another field, and winked at me.

Ryan came through the door and complimented me on what he thought was a job well done as he put his old leather briefcase down on the table. "They're really nice people aren't they?" he asked. "I always love it when we get to work with nice people... it makes our job so much more fulfilling when we can help people we like."

"Well our first job..." he said, taking the blue file in his hand, "is to narrow these down to the BEST three comparable sales, and the best three active listings, and then to see if there are any expired listings that might shed a little light on the matter."

"But won't all of the 20 properties I pulled up help us come to terms with the value of the property?" I asked. "Isn't too much information better than too little?"

"We're not going to ignore these sales Alan," said Ryan, "but Fred and Joan are looking to us to help them understand how much they can reasonably expect to sell the house for. I've always believed that to convince the Seller of value, we need to come up with an argument that will also convince a buyer."

"So you want to come up with a 'case' for the asking price? Something you would be prepared to stand in front of a buyer and argue?"

Ryan thought about it for a couple of seconds, rubbing his chin like he did when Joan was asking if she should fix things around the house. "That's a pretty good analogy. If we can't come up with a convincing argument for Joan and Fred, how can we possibly stand behind the listing price when negotiating with a buyer?'

"Good point. So why only three comparables then?" I asked.

"Simplicity. I'm a firm believer in the K.I.S.S. Principle," replied Ryan.

"Keep-It-Simple-Stupid?"

"Easy now," Ryan fired back. "I prefer Keep-It-Simply-Simple. But you get the gist. Too much information can clutter the mind and create confusion. We need to weed out the information that is a distraction. I've found that people's tolerance for data only allows them to really pay attention to three other properties and it's our job as experts to narrow the field."

"So how do you narrow them down?"

Ryan and I spent the next 30 minutes reviewing each of the properties that I thought shed light on what Joan and Fred's house may be worth. The first house we examined was located about a 20-minute drive from theirs, and so Ryan immediately put it to his left side. "This one's not bad," he said, "but it's a little farther away from the subject property than I'd like. Neighbourhoods can make a big difference in value." The next property was located just up the street from Joan and Fred's so I hoped it would make the cut.

"This one is a lot closer, but it's not waterfront. Alan, when you are looking for comparables, there are a few significant, subjective attributes that need to be reflected in the properties we choose," he said.

"Subjective?" I asked.

"Sure. Not all waterfront is created equal. And neither are all view properties. Just imagine how you would feel if I was helping you value your car. Wouldn't you question my opinion if I used a truck or an SUV as a comparable?"

"Well, I wouldn't say this property is THAT different from Joan and Fred's. It's just up the road and it has an awesome view of the same bay that Joan and Fred are on. Doesn't that count for something?"

"I guess if you could put a value on the view it might," he replied, sitting back in his chair. "How much is that view worth?"

"It's worth what someone is willing to pay for it, I guess."

"That's right," he said. "So if it's worth what someone is willing to pay for it, doesn't that mean that it's a subjective value?"

"Sure, but isn't every facet of a property subjective then?"

He returned to the information sheet on the comparable property. "Some things are, but not in such a definitive way. As you speak to more and more buyers, you'll find that they usually try and sum up what they are looking for in a brief sentence." Ryan changed the pitch of his voice and carried on, lifting his hand to his ear like a phone: "'Hi, we're looking for a view home to retire to for around $400,000.' Or 'I'm looking for a private, walk out waterfront property and the condition of the house really doesn't matter to me.' Or 'We're looking to purchase our first home and we're on a really tight budget, but we need it to have at least 3 bedrooms for our kids.'

He laughed at himself and carried on, "All of these descriptions touch on what helps to set the search criteria of buyers. We need to focus on the things that will differentiate the home from all the others in the minds of the buyers, and try and find comparable sales and listings that line up accordingly. Make sense?"

"I guess so," I said, a little deflated as the information sheet in his hand went into the "discard" pile on the right.

"We may return to some of these, if we aren't able to find better ones, but for now, let's keep looking." Ryan moved two more sheets into the pile on the right, claiming that they sold too long ago, leaving us with only 5 sheets left. I started to wonder if all my research time was wasted.

"Now this one's good," said Ryan, relieved. "When we're dealing with older homes and cottages, it's really hard to find great comparables, but this one fits the bill in a lot of ways."

"Finally! I didn't think we were going to find any and I was feeling pretty bad about leaving a copy of them all with Joan and Fred."

"Don't sweat it Alan," he said with a smile. "We'll just have to explain that sometimes even a truck and SUV can shed a little light on a car's value... I just haven't figured out how we'll do that!" We both chuckled but I knew that it would have to be me explaining my "newbie" mistake to Joan and Fred.

Ryan turned back to the property information sheet in his hand. "Can you pull the tax assessment value on this one, and its sales history Alan?"

As I made my way to the computer, Ryan used his red pen to circle things on the sheet.

"This house was built in 1972, but I know they did a major renovation back in the early 90's," Ryan said, not looking up. "While it's a little older than Joan and Fred's house, it 'plays' about the same age."

"So does that mean Joan and Fred's place is worth more since it was built in 1979?"

"I wouldn't apply a significant difference in value," he said. "Both houses appear to be structurally sound and I don't think an interested buyer would pay more or less for either because of the 7-year age difference."

"Fair enough. So when does age become a factor?" I asked.

"If you're comparing relatively new houses, a rough rule of thumb is to apply a 1% depreciation amount on the value of the improvements for every year, but there's a limit and the depreciation amount can be affected dramatically by how well the owners have taken care of the house."

"So two identical houses might be worth different amounts 10 years after they were built?"

"Absolutely," said Ryan. "If a house isn't maintained, it can have a dramatic impact on value. We would have to try and calculate how much it would cost to bring both homes into "like new" condition in order to try and determine how much the difference might be. Come to think of it, the amount it would cost to make a house "like new" is the amount of depreciation the house has suffered."

I thought about it and replied, "So the 1972 and the 1979 house would likely cost just as much to make "like new" and so the age difference doesn't really matter in this case?"

"Exactly," he said with a wink, turning back to the form in front of him. I watched as Ryan tapped the red pen on his teeth and squinted at the paper, reminding me of when I was studying so intensely for my Real Estate Licensing Exam.

"You look confused," I said.

"I am a little," he said, not looking away from the paper but pointing his pen to the sale price. "This place sold for about 10% more than I think it should have and it's thrown a wrench into what I thought was going to be my opinion of value."

"That ought to make Fred and Joan happy."

Ryan returned to tapping his lower teeth. "Not if it means they overprice their house and can't sell it," he muttered. Ryan flipped to the tax assessment value, circled the land value and the improvement values and leaned back in his chair.

"You see," he said, "the Assessor's value lines up with mine. They have it valued exactly where I would have said the market value was."

"But I thought you said we couldn't rely on the Assessed Value?"

"I wouldn't rely on it as necessarily an accurate reflection of market value, but it is a third party opinion of value that needs to be factored into the analysis. It's pretty unusual for the Assessors to be out by more than 10% either way, so at least it gives a good idea of the 'ballpark' we're playing in."

"So do property owners accept it as a reasonable value?" I asked. "It seems like buyers always ask about assessed value on properties that they are interest in. In fact, I'm starting to get pretty good at figuring out which properties people like best by the questions they ask about them."

"Good question... and a good observation," Ryan said putting down the papers and focusing on me as I sat back down at the table. "The reality is, most homeowners will have a preconceived notion of value in mind before you or I will ever speak with them and for some reason, the game becomes one of matching the value in their minds with the value in the market."

"I don't think I'm following you." I said. "I thought the reason we were looking for comparables was to try and determine the market value of the property, in a scientific way."

"Hmmm." Ryan paused. "Rather than thinking of this as a 'scientific' process, I'd think of it as more of a 'political' process. We need to take the information and facts at our disposal and develop an argument to support our position."

"So wouldn't it be helpful to know what Joan and Fred think the property is worth? Wouldn't that help us get the listing?"

"It very well would. But would you want the listing at an unreasonable price?"

"I guess it depends on how desperate I am for listings!?" I said truthfully.

"And therein lies one of the biggest challenges in our business Alan. You see, a rising market makes things easy on new Realtors® because eventually the market will catch up to an overpriced listing."

"So what's wrong with that? Doesn't the seller win by listing it high in that scenario?"

"Well, what would happen in Joan and Fred's situation if it took a long time to sell?" he asked, knowing full well the answer.

"I know, the price of the house they are moving to would go up. What if they were able to more than offset the amount of the increase of the house they buy into?"

"Outperform the market you mean?"

"Right. Outperform the market," I replied. "What if they staged the house and we put together an outstanding marketing package. Isn't it possible that we could get more money for their house?"

"Perhaps, but don't you think the sellers of the house that Joan and Fred will likely wind up buying will have the same ideas? It strikes me as a bit of a shell game."

"So why did that comparable property sell for 10% more than you thought it should? How do we tell Joan and Fred that their property shouldn't do the same?"

"That's a good question for Bill Porter. Give him a call please and see what you can find out about that sale."

"Really?" I asked. "Is that cool?" Bill Porter was a big name Realtor® in our market and sold a lot of properties with Ryan over the years. He had a reputation as a bit of a hard ass, but since he and Ryan had established a relationship over the years, they occasionally shared information even though they worked for different firms.

"Of course," Ryan replied. "I'd do the same for him. He doesn't have to tell us anything... but it never hurts to ask."

I had memorized the phone number for the other office and punched the number sequence into the phone. The receptionist answered and I was soon connected through to Bill Porter's cell phone.

"Bill Porter speaking."

"Hi Bill. It's Alan Stewart calling from Ryan's office and I wondered if I could ask you a question about the property you sold last year on Shale Crescent?"

"Hey Alan. Good to hear from you," he said, in less of a hurry than I would have expected. "I figured it was Ryan calling from this number. How is the ol' coot?"

"He's good, thanks, Bill. I'm sitting here with him now and he actually asked me to call you about this."

Bill laughed. "I wish I had someone to make my calls for me! Must be nice."

"I guess so," I replied, still feeling uneasy about having a "chat" with someone like Bill Porter, who had achieved a kind of Superhero status. "Ryan and I are doing an evaluation on a property in the area and we are hoping to use the Shale Crescent sale as a comparable."

"Uh-huh," said Bill, "You don't need my permission to do that."

"Well, we noticed that the property sold at full asking price and Ryan thought that the sale price was pretty high? Was there anything unusual about the sale, or do you think that was a good reflection of market value?"

"I get it Alan. I know the listing price was aggressive, but we wound up selling the property to the neighbour who had been trying to buy it privately for years. My client was a close personal friend of mine who knew exactly what he was prepared to sell it for and who knew that listing the property would put pressure on the neighbour to get realistic with his price," Bill explained. "Between you and me, we never had as much as a phone call on the property from anybody else."

"That explains a lot Bill. Hang on a second," I said, putting my hand over the receiver as Ryan gestured to me.

"Tell him we will let him know about the new listing as soon as we can to return the favour," Ryan whispered.

"Bill, Ryan wants you to know you'll be the first to know if we get this new listing. Thanks for all your help."

"That's great Alan. Good luck!" Bill said as the phone line clicked dead. Ryan congratulated me on making the call and we both agreed that without having done so, we easily could have put too much emphasis on this sale, skewing Joan and Fred's expectations. I feared that I may have already done so as a result of leaving them with the information I did, which included the Shale Crescent sale. *Live and learn.*

We spent the next 20 minutes finalizing the best three comparable sales, the best three active listings and two expired listings. Ryan put his red pen to work on each of them, circling the things that we needed to pay attention to and making notes about why they were worth more or less than the subject property.

"This one has a detached garage," he said, not looking up from the paper. "Our neighbours had a detached garage like this one built last year and it cost them about $35,000, so that's got to come off of this one."

"This house is a great comparable," he continued, "but the property faces north and doesn't get much sun. Tough to put a number on that, but it's definitely a knock against it. I'm going to say it's worth $30,000 but the reality is, some people won't even consider it if they're looking for lots of sun."

"The land value on this one and Joan and Fred's is likely identical, but the house is almost 400 square feet bigger and has an extra bathroom. Given the age and quality of construction, I'd say $150 a square foot is a reasonable adjustment amount for the extra space, so that means we have to subtract $60,000 from their asking price..." Ryan paused to do some math on the scratch pad beside him and then said triumphantly, "Which puts it right in line with the other properties we're looking at."

Ryan pieced everything together like a puzzle, and it was obvious that he enjoyed the process. On a pre-printed worksheet that he retrieved from his briefcase, he started to fill in the blanks.

"Average Adjusted Comparative Value: Solds - $349,500. Average Adjusted Comparative Value: Actives - $358,000. BC Assessment Authority Value: $329,000..." He sat back in his chair for a moment before commenting again, then leaned forward and wrote two more figures into the worksheet: "Opinion of Value: $345,000 - $365,000!"

"Is that about what you expected the property to be worth?" I asked, curious about how much influence his initial estimate would factor into his deductions.

"Spot on actually. I wondered if we could push it over $380,000, but I think paints a pretty clear picture that Joan and Fred will likely be frustrated if we price it at anything above $374,500."

"That's a lot less than the one on Shoal Crescent. I hope I didn't set their expectations too high."

"All you did was provide them with information Alan, and that's never a bad thing. We can now provide more clarity for them and they will have to draw their own conclusions. Now all that's left to do is package it all up in a Comparative Market Analysis and present it."

"I'll get on it," I said, taking the stack of papers from in front of him and heading to the computer to start preparing my first CMA using the template I had helped the team create since my arrival.

THE CMA

PUTTING IT ALL TOGETHER

As the hard drive whirred to life I made a fresh pot of coffee and looked out over the ocean, taking a moment to enjoy this new job, my new colleagues and the blessing of working alongside someone like Ryan. I thought to myself: *There is no way I could have pulled this all together with nearly as much accuracy if it weren't for Ryan. There is simply no replacement for experience and knowledge! I would have encouraged Joan and Fred to list for at least $25,000 more... which, in hindsight, would have been bad for everyone.*

I returned to the computer and opened the CMA Template in our Word Processing Program. A bright and colourful, but professional-looking, cover page set the tone for the rest of the document. Along with a professional photograph of our team members and our company logo, there was a blank frame into which I would have to insert a photo of Joan and Fred's home. I opened the file folder that I had created earlier for the property and double clicked on the folder marked 'Photos.' A window opened with all the images I had captured during our meeting the previous day and I selected the photo that best captured the 'story' of the property.

I scrolled down to review the second page, a page that had taken me most of a day to create. At the top of the page was written in large, but comfortable script, "About Our Team" and seeing it took me back to the day that Ryan and I spent coming to terms with who we were as a team with Kim and Ryan's old friend and client, John Duma:

"We are a team of caring real estate professionals who help our customers turn their dreams into reality by providing invaluable advice, proven marketing strategies and expert negotiating skills."

As a result of being involved in the process we had been through together, I knew I could speak with authority and conviction about why our team was the right team for the job.

I used a PDF editor to insert the comparable properties' data sheets into the appropriate sections of the CMA and filled hit the SAVE button to store it into Joan and Fred's folder on the harddrive before printing the package out and binding it.

Turning off the lights in the office, I headed for home, excited about what tomorrow would bring.

PRESENTING THE CMA

Ryan and I met at his office the following morning and shared the car ride to Joan and Fred's home. I was confident that the work we had done the day before had helped me come to terms with my very best estimate of market value.

"Ryan, I've learned a lot over the past couple of days about developing some kind of scientific evaluation of Joan and Fred's house but I've also learned that there are some things you can't assign a specific value to." I said. " At the end of the day, it seems to me that a house is really worth what someone is willing to pay for it."

"That's a great way to sum it up Alan," Ryan replied. "So does that mean you aren't going to be able to give Joan and Fred an accurate market value of their house?"

"No, I'm comfortable in supporting the value you and I have come up with, but I think it's important to let Joan and Fred know that there is a chance the market may bear more than what we are going to tell them," I paused. "I really feel responsible to not steer them wrong in their decision on what to list the property at."

Ryan scratched his beard for a second or two and then replied, "So who determines the asking price for the home if you are going to list it for sale."

"Well, ultimately it's Joan and Fred's decision, I guess."

"Why do you say that?" Ryan asked, setting me up.

"Because it's their place to sell. If they don't like my price, they can always list with somebody else."

"That's true. But don't you have something to say about it?"

"Sure," I said with a laugh, "but I want to list their house so I can sell it and feed my family."

"So would you list it at 50% over market value?" he said, looking at me while I kept my eyes on the road.

"Of course not."

Ryan looked back out the front windshield. "Why not?"

"Because that would be a waste of my time and money," I replied. "At that price no one would even look at the property."

"Why not?"

"Because there isn't anyone that would see value in a property at 50% over market value."

I could tell Ryan was pleased with himself.

"So would you list it at 25% higher than what we have agreed is the market value of the property?"

"I still don't think it would be worth the time and energy... and besides, Bill would laugh at me for taking on the listing at that price."

"Oh really?" said Ryan, now laughing a little himself. "I've seen ol' Bill take some listings at more inflated prices than that!"

I thought it would be a good time to turn the tables. "So tell me Ryan, would you list it at 10% over what we've suggested?"

"Probably," he said without an explanation.

"Really? We've decided the place is probable worth $350,000 and you're telling me you would list the place for $385,000?" I said, surprised. "That seems like way more than anyone would pay for the place."

"Alan, the last thing I want to do is to encourage you to list homes at more than they we can say they are worth using all the resources at our disposal," said Ryan, somewhat apologetically. "But we've got a business to run. The market is active, our listing inventory is low, and there are a million subjective things about this property that factor into the valuation. All I can tell you is that I believe there is one person out there that would be willing to pay $385,000 for this property if we market it properly."

I didn't reply for a while, which seemed to make us both uncomfortable. Ryan had just contradicted most everything I had learned during my licensing course... but it made perfect sense.

"But in my licensing course we were taught that taking overpriced listings was a surefire way to increase your expenses and your frustration level."

Ryan, appreciating my internal conflict carried on. "Please don't think that I'm encouraging you to over inflate your evaluation on the property to get the listing Alan. That wouldn't be doing a service to anyone. But if Joan and Fred aren't prepared to list the home for sale at the price you recommend, you're going to be faced with a challenge and a decision."

"Okay?"

"Your challenge is going to be to find out what price they ARE prepared to list at, and your decision is whether or not it's worth taking the listing."

"But do you think they would consider listing with me if I insult them with a valuation that's way lower than they are expecting?"

"That's why you've done all your homework," Ryan said with a smile. "So long as you can support your position, no one can take offense. The only time people take offense is when you pull a number out of thin air and it doesn't line up with what they have in mind."

Ryan and I pulled up in front of Joan and Fred's place and by the time we had stepped out of the car Joan had already pushed open the screen door and was waiting to greet us. I couldn't help but hum a little tune to myself... *Don't sweat it, you're going to get it!* I smiled a little at that.

"Good morning gentlemen," Joan said with a smile. "Right on time!"

"Good morning Joan," I replied, taking the weight of the spring loaded door from her and allowing her to retreat into the cabin with Ryan following right behind. "What a beautiful day!"

"It sure is," she replied. "I've got to tell you that it's mornings like this that I wonder if we're doing the right thing by selling."

"I can see why!" said Ryan. "The view from here is spectacular when the sun is flooding the bay."

Without asking, Joan poured a cup of coffee for each of us and a fourth, presumably for Fred. "What do you take in your coffee Ryan?"

"Just a little milk please Joan."

"And you Alan?"

"I'll have mine black, thanks."

"I'll take mine with cream! None of that skim milk for me," said Fred as he came up the stairs. "How are you boys this morning?"

"Great thanks, Fred." I said, accepting his outreached hand. "Good to see you."

"You too." he said, breaking our handshake and extending another to Ryan. "So have you figured out how many millions we can expect to get for this place?"

"Good morning Fred," replied Ryan with a wink. "At least a couple of million!"

Joan invited us all to sit at the kitchen table and I positioned myself beside Ryan with Joan and Fred sitting to my right. I wanted to be sure to be able to speak to the two of them together and not have to bounce back and forth between them.

A little nervous, I led off. "Joan and Fred, I want to let you know that regardless of how you decide to move forward, I'm really honoured that you have called me to help you sell your house. It means a lot to me. With that said, I want to talk to you about a few things before we turn to my evaluation of your property. Would that be alright with you?"

"Of course Alan," said Joan in a serious tone.

I continued, remembering what Ryan had told potential listing clients in dozen listing presentations that I had joined him in. "There are really three things that home sellers hire a real estate agent for. First, you hire them to help you understand the value of your house. Do you agree?"

They both nodded.

"The second thing that you hire them to do is market it effectively. To get photographs, floor plans and prepare a marketing message and marketing plan that presents the property in its best light to as many prospective clients as possible. Does that make sense?"

"Sure thing," said Fred while Joan continued to nod.

"And finally, you hire an agent to help you negotiate the very best deal on your behalf and make sure the deal closes. Can we agree that helping you come to terms with value, marketing the house and providing expert negotiating skills are the primary criteria for which you would base your hiring decision when selecting a Realtor®?"

"I think so Alan," said Joan. "But what is really important to me is that we can trust that person to take care of us on all of those items."

"I appreciate that Joan. What I want to be sure is that if you do decide to sell your house, that you won't just focus on my evaluation in making your decision. Can I tell you why?"

"Of course," said Fred, who seemed to be getting a little impatient.

"It's a two-fold answer Fred," I paused for a second to be sure I remembered what I was going to say, which actually worked well for dramatic effect. "First, while I wish I had a crystal ball, the market is fluid and changes depending on the number of buyers who may be competing for a certain type of property, the number of other suitable properties that those buyers might consider, and myriad of external factors including the economy, bank rates and economic forecasts. What I will try and do today is share with you what I recommend as a listing price based on all the information available, but at the end of the day the market will bear what it will bear."

"OK, that makes sense Alan," said Fred.

"The second reason I recommend not focusing solely on the evaluation is that when people are making a decision on which Realtor® to use, the recommended listing price is the one variable that an agent can use to manipulate a homeowner's decision without ever having to deliver any other service or skill to effect the desired result... which is of course selling your home at the highest price in the shortest amount of time." I paused to see if Joan and Fred were following. "In other words, if you were comparing me with two other Realtors® and all other things being equal, if I suggested you could sell your house for X and the other two Realtors® told you that you could sell your house for X minus 10%, human nature would suggest you should list with me in order to maximize your return."

"But why would an agent give us a price that's too high to sell Alan?" asked Joan. "That seems counter intuitive if what they want to do is sell it to make a commission."

"From the Realtors® standpoint, there is an advantage to having the listing even if it takes months to sell. Imagine you owned a store with nothing on the shelf Joan." I paused to let that sink in. "Wouldn't it be better to have something on the shelf you could negotiate the sale of than nothing at all? Wouldn't a shopper be more likely to come into the store filled with product than one with empty shelves? Having listings is an important part of every Realtors® business, even though the strategy may not line up with satisfying the needs of the property owner."

"But Alan, put yourself in our shoes for a minute," said Fred. "If one agent thinks my house is more valuable than another, then I would say he's more likely to negotiate a better price for us at the end of the day."

"Perhaps," I replied. "But if that agent doesn't have the ability to market the home effectively and isn't a skilled negotiator or leaves holes in the contract that leave you unprotected, does it really matter how much he thinks your home is worth? I'm not saying that you don't want to hire a Realtor® who sees all the value in your home, but don't make that the reason you hire someone."

"I see your point." he conceded.

Ryan chimed in, "Alan and I were speaking about the matter this morning and I thought Alan had a very valid point when he suggested that a house is really worth what someone is willing to pay for it. So for me, the most important part in selling a home for its highest value is to present the house in its best possible light to the widest number of people. From there, the market will do its work."

Joan, looking a little more serious than we started, interjected, "I'm getting the feeling you're going to tell us some bad news about what you think we should be selling for?"

"Not at all Joan," I said to her in my most reassuring tone. "I just want you to know that if you do decide to list your house for sale, we will need to work together as a team. Our estimate of market value and what the house may sell for are two different things. We've tried to determine the market value using a scientific method, but how we pricing it for sale is more of an art than a science. We always need to factor your needs and motivation as well. Does that make sense?"

"Yes it does," said Fred. "So now can you tell us how much it's worth!? You're killing me here."

"Just one more thing. It's a question that Ryan has taught me to ask so that we are all on the same page when it comes to our intentions." I looked directly at Fred, which was hard but important. "Fred, if we can come to terms on an appropriate listing price for your home today and you're satisfied that we are able to deliver an effective marketing plan and negotiate expertly on your behalf, is there any reason that Ryan and I won't have earned your business?"

"I don't think so Alan, but as you know the numbers all have to work for us."

"Okay then," I continued. "Let's have a look at the conclusions I've come to in my Comparative Market Analysis."

I finally pushed the evaluation that I'd kept my hand on the whole time onto the table in front of Fred and Joan.

"Now there a couple of parts to this evaluation. The first part is information on what makes our team special and how we plan on marketing your home."

We spent a few minutes reviewing each of the bullet points on the "Meet the Team" and "Our Marketing Plan" pages of the CMA knowing that I would certainly lose Fred's attention the moment we talked about what we felt his home was worth... particularly if our number fell short of what his expectations were.

"So now that you know what we bring to the table, let's look at what we feel your home is worth," I said as Joan and Fred both leaned forward on the table. "Remember, neither Ryan or I are appraisers, and while we are prepared to defend our opinion of value, this isn't a certified appraisal."

"Do we need one?" asked Joan.

"It's completely up to you Joan." said Ryan. "An appraisal can go a long way to satisfying buyers of the value in a property, but it isn't necessary for listing your home for sale if you are confident in the information we present you today."

I carried on. "We've drawn our conclusions from a number of sources. First, we've analyzed the changes in the market since you've purchased the home and included a factor for the improvements you've made and a factor for the depreciation of the buildings. This is an objective way for us to start drilling down towards today's value." Joan and Fred both nodded, accepting this approach as reasonable. "Then we look at recent sales and active listings of properties that are comparable to yours as well as properties that failed to sell."

"Why would you care about properties that didn't sell?" asked Joan.

"Because they help us to determine where the price ceiling for your house may be Joan," I replied, focusing my attention on her. "We focus primarily on the houses that have sold to determine what the market value may be, and we focus on the active listings and the expired listings that didn't sell to help us price the home competitively. Does that make sense?"

"Perfectly," she replied. "So what you're saying is that there is a difference between what our house might be worth and how we price it for sale? I hadn't thought about the two things being different before."

"Exactly. Like I was saying, pricing the house is more of an art than a science." I turned to Fred. "In a rising market, it wouldn't make sense to look only at past sales to determine the asking price, would it?"

"No. But like Ryan said yesterday, the more the market goes up, the more it's going to cost us to make this move."

"Bingo," I said, turning my attention back to Joan and noticing a satisfied grin on Ryan's face. "That's why pricing the house properly means we all have to work together. If you were downsizing, it might make a lot of sense to price the property high and wait for the market to catch up to it, but in your case, I think we may be better off pricing it in a way that attracts a lot of attention and maybe even multiple offers."

We turned our attention back to the package of information compiled in the CMA.

Using Third Party Values: The HPI and Average Price Graphs

"So let's start with the market changes," I said, flipping to the 10 Year Home Price Index graph for the local market. "The Home Price Index is designed to show the changes in the value of a home over time. It's an index, not an average, so it's designed to help us to determine the rise and fall in values, rather than show us how much people are spending on homes. The average and median price are both affected by activity levels in certain price ranges, but the index is supposed to reflect what has happened to the value of a home over time, and it isn't affected by the number of expensive or inexpensive houses that sell. Does that make sense?"

Joan and Fred looked confused.

Ryan helped out. "If lots of expensive homes are selling, it will increase the average and median values, but it doesn't mean that a particular home is worth any more or less. If the lower end of the market is active, it will bring average and median prices down regardless of whether or not the value of a particular home has risen, fallen or stayed the same."

"So how do the 'experts' determine the index Ryan?" asked Fred, looking a bit sceptical.

"I'd be lying if I told you I understood it all," said an embarrassed Ryan, "but I can tell you that in my experience over the past 12 years it has been a reliable tool. I trust the economists and analysts that have put it together."

I carried on, turning to the HPI graph in my CMA package. "What we know is that you bought your house 5 years ago come September, so I've noted the Housing Price Index at that time, which was $145,000." I pulled a red pen from my jacket pocket and circled the number.

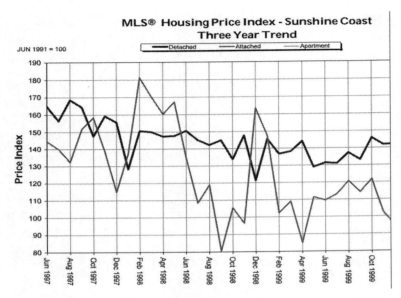

PHOTO CREDIT: REAL ESTATE BOARD OF GREATER VANCOUVER

"And today the housing market is set at $185,000." Another red circle. "That's an increase of 27.5%."

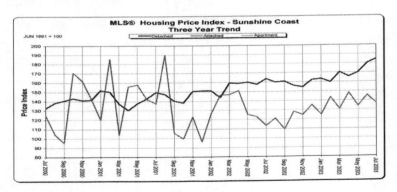

PHOTO CREDIT: REAL ESTATE BOARD OF GREATER VANCOUVER

"Well that's good news," said Joan, looking a bit more at ease.

"Yes, that's a healthy increase Joan," I agreed. "Maybe not as big a rise as you may have realized with your house in the city, but a pretty reasonable return on your investment. Now, since then you've also built the shed out back, resurfaced the sundeck and made a really impressive change in your bedroom and master bath. All those things have added value. In my opinion, those improvements have added about $20,000 to the value of the home."

"I like that number Alan," said Fred. "We only spent about $15,000 doing all that work."

"Good for you. That's another win." I smiled. "Now we have to remember that the buildings, the roof and the appliances are all 5 years older than when you bought the house, and so we've made an adjustment of $10,000 to account for the depreciation of those assets."

"But the appliances are fine and there's no issues with the roof. I don't think we should have to discount them," said Joan.

Ryan touched her arm and said "Joan, think of it this way. In a condominium, owners pay strata fees every month to cover the cost of ongoing repairs and to build up their contingency fund to cover unexpected costs and major projects. It's a monthly expense. You have been able to enjoy a leak free roof, functioning hot water tank, and all your appliances for the last 5 years, but they all have a life expectancy. It's only reasonable to factor in the depreciation of the major systems of the house if you are going to include the improvements. And remember, this is a way of trying to come up with a subjective opinion of value."

Joan accepted the explanation, unhappily, and I carried on. "Now looking back at the sales history, this home was listed at $285,000 and you paid $277,000. Does that sound right?"

Fred nodded. "Yes, the ol' timer we bought it from was a tough negotiator, but the place had been on the market for almost two months, so we were able to get the price down a little."

"OK then. So if you paid what could be considered to be fair market value, we can multiply what you paid for the home by the same increase in the Housing Price Index. $277,000 x 1.275 = $353,175. And if we add in the $20,000 worth of improvements and subtract the $10,000 worth of depreciation, the Housing Price Index would suggest your house should be worth somewhere in or around $360,000 today. Does that seem reasonable to you?"

"Well, it's certainly in the range," said Fred, shedding some light on the value Joan and he put on the property and giving me hope that my analysis would line up with their expectations.

Taking another play out of Ryan's playbook I wrote in relatively large letters:

"Based on HPI, Suggested Market Value $360,000."

COMPARABLES

"Now that we've got some context around what has happened to the value of your property over time, based on the housing price index, we're ready to start looking at the comparable properties to help us gain even more insights as to an appropriate price to list your home for sale." Seeing little interest in waiting from Joan or Fred, I carried on. "First, we'll have a look at the properties that have sold recently."

"Now I need you to know," injected Ryan, "that Alan and I really worked hard to find the very best comparable sales to use."

"Ryan is right," I confessed, knowing that Ryan was giving me an opportunity to discuss the fact that one of the comparable sales I had left with them the day before was inappropriate. "Joan, yesterday I left a number of data sheets with you, and after Ryan and I review them we agreed that one of them may actually mislead you."

"I bet I know exactly which one it is," said Joan. "It's that house on Stone Road, isn't it?"

I leaned back in my chair. "Well how did you know that?"

"It just didn't seem to fit in with the others," Fred said. "We talked about it for a long time last night and we thought maybe it was a mistake."

"Well, we all make mistakes," I said with a nervous laugh. "While that house has a lot of comparable features, it's lacking one major component that we just weren't able to add subjective value to. Even though it's in the same neighborhood I was wrong to provide you a non-waterfront comparable, and that's why we removed it from the evaluation."

"So which houses did you find to be good comparables?"

"There were three houses that sold last year that all help us come to an idea of what your house might be worth Joan." I flipped the pages in the CMA to get to them. "I've put the very best of them at the front of our package."

Just like when reviewing the Housing Price Index, I picked up my pen and readied it to highlight the important parts of the feature sheet that I had printed off.

"This property is located just around the corner and sold 35 days ago for $374,500. You may have known the old owners, the Smiths?"

"Yes, we actually had dinner with the Smiths last year," said Joan. "They were thinking of selling then, but didn't have it on the market."

"Right. They came on the market a little over 3 months ago and the property sold in couple of months, which gives us some confidence that it had lots of exposure to the market and sold for fair market value." We returned to the paperwork. "In breaking down the value, the first thing we do is to look at the land value and either add or subtract from the price depending on how they line up. This property is 20% larger than your property and faces due south, but the waterfront is higher bank which is a detraction." I circled the lot size and the orientation on the page. "As a result, we feel the land under this house is worth more than your property, so while we won't assign a particular amount just yet, I'm just going to put big plus sign here beside the lot size."

Fred looked puzzled and directed his question to Ryan, "Why wouldn't you add value to that now?"

Ryan replied, "At this point Fred we are dealing with the artistic or subjective part of the evaluation. This is where we take all the information and use our experience and expertise to help us really try and unravel the whole picture about your property. At the end of the day all we can really say is that a buyer would likely pay more for this lot than they would for yours."

I continued. "Now we turn our attention to the house. As you can see, this home is 500 square feet bigger than yours." Red circle with a plus. "And offers a third bathroom downstairs." Red circle with a plus. "There is a drilled well and septic field just like your place," (Red circle) "but what the comparable property doesn't have is the charm and character of your place." Big red circle around the write up and a minus sign.

"I agree Alan. That place was so boring and really needed a woman's touch. So does that offset the other factors?" asked Joan.

"I don't think it does completely Joan, but it sure helps," I said. "If I were working with buyers considering buying this property or yours, I would say your house was worth somewhere in or around $30,000 less than this one. Which would put a comparable value on your home of around $355,000." I always rounded up when looking at comparables so that the homeowner knew that I was on their side!

"That seems about right," said Fred. "But don't forget the Housing Price Index shows that prices have gone up last month."

"Good point," I said scratching out the $355,000 and putting in $357,500. "Better?"

"Much," said Fred.

"Great, let's look at the other two comparable properties."

We spend another 5 minutes or so looking at the other two best SOLD comparables.

"So now that we have adjusted the 3 comparables based on the similarities or differences to your property, we simply add up the three values and divide by three to give ourselves an average SOLD comparable market value, which is..." I punched the series of numbers into my calculator and totalled it, divided by three and read the result allowed, "$359,500. Does that seem about right to you?"

"That's a little less than we thought after looking at the comparables you left us last night," said Joan, "but don't you think that's fair Fred?"

"Ya. Obviously we want to get as much as possible, but it's fair."

"Well there is only one way to find out what someone will pay, and that's to list it for sale." I replied. "But let's have a quick look at what the properties that are for sale now would suggest we could list it for. If we don't have enough information by then we can always look at the expired listings."

"Fair enough," said Fred, not lifting his eyes from the CMA package in front of him.

I flipped ahead a couple of pages to the first Active Listing Comparable.

"Now this house is actually also in my Expired Listings section because it didn't sell when it came on the market 3 months ago, so they relisted it for sale at this new price of $355,000."

"I know that house," said Fred. "We paddle past it when we kayak out of the bay. It's a really dark property."

"That's right. I've shown it to lots of prospective buyers who love how it looks in the ads but who say the same thing when they are actually on the property." I circled the orientation section of the data sheet which noted 'North Facing' and put a minus sign beside it. "It also looks directly across the bay, and doesn't have nearly as nice an outlook as yours." I put another minus sign beside the photo of the view.

"You should also know that they've reduced the price from $365,000 when they first relisted it," added Ryan.

"So how do you think we stack up against this one?" asked Joan.

"Well, if I took buyers to this house and they knew the price was $355,000 and then I brought them to your house, my guess is they would assume yours would be priced at $375,000 or more." I wrote 'Comparable Value - $377,500' and circled it on the top of the page.

We went through the same exercise for the other two comparable active listings before averaging the prices at $374,900.

"That's better," said Joan, looking excited about moving forward.

Without referring to the Expired Listings I flipped to the part of our CMA that was titled Suggested Market Value and started writing in red ink as I said, "I don't know about you, but based on your tax assessment at $340,000, the Housing Price Index value of $360,000, and the comparison to sales at $359,000 I think it's safe to say your house has a current market value of somewhere between $350,000 and $370,000." I looked up to make sure I had agreement from Fred and Joan who weren't putting up any arguments. I returned to the page and signed it for effect.

"But how much would you suggest we list it for Alan?" asked Joan.

"Well, given what we know about the other houses on the market now and how much your property is likely worth, what do you think we should list if for Joan?"

Joan looked at Fred, "What do you think about $369,000 Fred?"

"I was thinking more like $375,000," replied Fred as he crossed his arms. I don't want to be too greedy but we can always come down. Right Ryan?"

Ryan leaned in towards Fred and said in a reassuring tone, "Fred and Joan, we would be proud to represent the property for sale at $375,000, but my sincere advice given your circumstances is to list it at $369,000 and hold tighter to your price during negotiations."

I jumped into the conversation. "And don't forget Fred that we agreed your current competition would suggest a listing price of

$375,000, so if we want to stand out as being good value in this market, a price of $369,000 should attract more attention."

Fred conceded. "All right, $369,900 then."

"I've got the paperwork right here!" I said, probably a little too excited as I pulled a blue listing folder from my bag.

Twenty minutes later Ryan and I were pulling out of their driveway and heading back to the office. I could feel Ryan looking at me and I just couldn't contain the huge satisfied grin that spread across my face.

"Don't sweat it… I GOT MY FIRST LISTING!" I said out loud.

We both laughed and Ryan patted my leg with his left hand. "Well done boy. Well done."

LISTING THE PROPERTY

When we got back to the office Kim looked up with a curious glare at me. "Well?"

I pulled the blue folder out from behind my back and rang the brass bell beside the door. "We got it!"

"Good for you Mr. Stewart!" Kim said, reaching out a hand for a high five. "I knew you'd get it."

"Alan did a really good job Kim," said Ryan. "He gave Joan and Fred everything they needed to make an informed decision, and listed the property at a great price. I was impressed."

"With no small thanks to you Ryan," I added. "I know that if we weren't working together I would have had a very hard time convincing Fred to list with a rookie. Thanks for being there."

"Alan, I wouldn't have missed it for the world."

I sat down at my desk and pulled the "Listing Checklist" from the file.

Listing Checklist / Information Sheet

Listing Date		Expiry Date		
Name (1)		☐Primary	Cell	☐Text OK
email			Other	
Name (2)		☐Primary	Cell	☐Text OK
email			Other	
Property Address				
Mailing Address				
Showing Instructions				

Checklist

Agency Brochure, PCDS, FINTRAC & Listing Agreement	Prepare Ad Copy ☐ Client's Approved
Copy of Documents to Seller or Access to Online Folder	Prepare Feature Sheet w/ floor plan ☐ Client's Approved
Home Measurements and Floor Plan Ordered	Listing Package Provided to Office
Photos Ordered / Taken	For Sale Sign Installed ☐ Ordered ☐ Custom Rider
Obtain Keys / Lockbox Code or Key #:	Date for Agents Open:
Complete Data Input Sheet	Date for Public Open:
Taxes and Title Confirmed / Charges Ordered	Order Just Listed Postcards and distribute
Obtain Strata Plan / Lot Plan	Contact REALTORS with nearby listings
Obtain Financials and Bylaws (Strata)	Review MLS Input for any errors
Listing on Sales Board in Office	Launch Social Media Campaign

Upon Accepted Offer / **Upon Firm Sale**

Transaction Record Sheet to Office	Subject Removal to Office
Contract and Deposit to Office	Buyer's Lawyer:
Deposit Increase date:	Seller's Lawyer:
Mortgage Approved By:	Referral Form (if applicable)
Strata Docs by date:	Install SOLD sign
Inspections by date:	Order Change of Address Cards for Sellers
Other Subjects by date:	Order Just Sold Postcards and distribute

Immediately Prior to Closing

Remove Sign	Call Clients to ensure document signing completed
Purchase closing gift	Arrange for keys to buyers and possession instructions
Meet Buyers and Agent on Possession Date	Deliver Client Gift 2 days after possession

(See Appendix G Listing Checklist)

I started at the top and went through the list so that I could give everything to Kim to process. I put my initials beside everything I needed to do. Because I had taken our prepared listing folder and gone through the paperwork in order, I had completed everything

191

I needed for Kim except for the MLS Data sheet which I had put off until I returned to take photos of the house after Joan and Fred had a chance to get their homework done. I scanned the rest of the page to see what was left for Kim to do. Satisfied that I had done all I could for the time being I passed the file over to Kim.

"Here's the first of many!" I said, puffed up from the morning's success. "Over to you."

It had been a draining couple of days and I decided to go home for an extended lunch. I walked in the front door of our home to find Paola and our daughters Mackenzie and Samantha playing with bright coloured plastic blocks on the floor, building what looked to be a house.

"Daddy's home!" Paola said as she stood up to greet me with a hug. "Look what your girls are making for you Daddy. A house to sell."

I took to the floor with our daughters, giving them both a kiss on head. "Well this is beautiful ladies." They looked pleased.

"I'm building a house Daddy," said 6-year-old Mackenzie. "But don't sell it. It's for us! Okay?"

"Okay sweetheart, I promise I won't sell it." We started working on it together and Paola joined in as well.

"So how did things go this morning with Fred and Joan?" Paola asked. "Did they list their house?"

I couldn't contain the smile that came across my face. I had planned on announcing my big success with a celebratory toast at the dinner table, but it was too obvious. "They did list it... WITH ME!"

"That's fantastic Honey. We're so proud of you!"

Samantha stood up on her 4-year-old legs and skipped over to me, wrapped her arms around me, and said "I'm pwoud of you Daddy."

I don't think Samantha had any idea of what had transpired, but she had fun sharing the same words I would say to her every night as we tucked her into bed.

"I'm proud of myself too," I replied. "Today some of our friends told me how much they trusted me by letting me help them sell their house. It means a lot to me."

Samantha gave me another squeeze and then fell to the floor with a thud, returning to our project with her sister.

"So what's next?" asked Paola.

"Well, we have a couple of days to get everything in order. Joan and Fred are working on the list of things that Ryan and I recommended they get done before we put the house on the market, but we don't want to wait too long to get the place listed."

"Is there anything I can do to help?"

"You know," I said, grateful for the help, "what might be nice would be to make one of your lasagnas. Joan's got a pretty big to do list, and I'm sure taking care of a couple of meals for them would be a real blessing."

"That's a great idea. I was going to make one for us anyway, so I'll just double up the recipe."

I spent another 10 minutes building our dream home with the girls before I heard their little sister wake up from her nap. I made my way into her room and her face lit up when she saw me.

"Dada!"

I picked Hannah up from her crib and gave her a big hug. "Daddy's had a big day sweetheart. A really big day."

CHAPTER 6

RYAN'S PATH

O n arriving at work early one Monday morning, I was surprised to find Ryan sitting at the meeting table with a cup of coffee in front of him and a smile on his face. No journal or day timer. No newspaper or real estate magazine. Just a big grin on his face and his coffee.

"What's gotten into you?" I asked. "You look like a kid on Christmas morning."

"I feel like a kid on Christmas morning," he replied before having a big swig of his coffee. "Can I show you something?"

I put my bag at my desk and my lunch in the fridge and Ryan and I headed to his car.

"So what's the big surprise?" I asked, intrigued by what could make Ryan so excited.

"It's not really a surprise," Ryan said, looking straight ahead. "In fact, you've seen this place before. The surprise is what I'm going to tell you about it."

"So cryptic," I said.

As we drove along the familiar road that led to our local village and past a large stretch of trees and that separated where we were from a local fishing hole called Pack Lake, Ryan turned on his signal light and made a left turn down a driveway on a property we had listed for sale. The property had been challenging to sell as a result of the distance between the road and the lake, the cost of development and servicing a building site so far away, and an awkward park dedication that ran 50' up from the edge of the lake, making the waterfront accessible, but with no assurance of privacy in the long run.

The municipality had accepted the park dedication from the owner as compensation for another subdivision that the owner had applied for years before, at a time when Pack Lake waterfront wasn't of much value. While the trout fishing was great, the peaty lake wasn't big enough for boating and the leeches meant it wasn't of much use for swimming.

"So what gives? Did you finally sell this place?" I asked, assuming Ryan was just being glib about selling such a difficult property.

"Nope," he replied, stopping and applying the emergency brake in the middle of a large clearing. "I bought it."

"You bought it?" I asked, surprised to say the least. "What for?"

"Alan, I'm going to build a retirement community right here and you are going to help me sell it."

"A retirement community?" I asked, still in shock. "But the property is only zoned for two homes."

"That's right. But the Municipality has been looking for affordable housing options, particularly for the elderly, and they have agreed to work with me in getting this off the ground."

We spent the next few minutes making our way down a narrow trail to the waterfront. The property, logged 7 years earlier, was thick with Alder trees but as we walked Ryan pointed to different parts of the lot and described his plans.

"The park dedication is perfect! We will have 7 duplex homes lining the waterfront here," he said with his arms set out in front of him, "but everyone will have access to Pack Lake. We'll have a dock over here with canoes and kayaks for people to use." Ryan turned sharply to the left with his hands still in front of him. "We'll have 7 homes on the top side of the property facing South with views of the lake," he said, turning another 180 degrees, "and 7 homes on the lower section of the property that will look over a greenbelt. Back near the road we'll also have an activity centre with a workshop and gathering space."

"Wow," I said, sincerely. "When did this all come about? We spend virtually every day together Ryan and you've never told me about any of this."

"It's something Sue and I have wanted to do for a long time Alan, but we had to find the right property. On Thursday night it hit me. I was lying in bed doing a mental inventory of every property I could think of that would fit the bill and which would allow us to build 15 – 20 homes. When I realized that there was simply nothing that was already zoned for multi-family construction, I decided I had to simply think of what would offer the acreage I would require and then get to work on figuring out how to rezone it. It was then that I realized I had been trying to sell the perfect piece of property for the last 12 months!"

"So you bought it without even knowing if you can rezone it?" I asked.

"Well I haven't bought it, but I have come to terms with Mr. Katz, the owner, and negotiated a 90-day due diligence period which should give me enough time to determine whether or not I'm prepared to take the risk on completing on the purchase."

"But you're so busy already," I said, "how are you going to find the time to do all this?"

"That's where you come in my boy," he said, with the same Christmas morning grin returning to his face. "I'm going to pass the torch to you. I want you to have my real estate business, and in return, I want you to help me with the marketing of this project. What do you say?"

I was speechless. It was less than 6 months since I had started working with Ryan and here he was offering me what had taken him 12 years to create. "Uh... I don't know, Ryan. I'm flattered, but I'm not sure I'm ready to take this on by myself."

"You won't be alone Alan. I've been able to give it a fair amount of thought this weekend, and I think I have a strategy that will work for everyone."

We walked back to the car and Ryan continued to explain his plans for the property but all I could think about was the fact that his heart had left our business over the weekend and that unless things didn't work out on this property, I would be flying solo in as little as 90 days. My heart raced, and my stomach sank, but the rest is history.

Thanks to Ryan's teaching and mentoring, I would go on to build one of the most satisfying and lucrative careers I could have ever imagined. With the help of my partner, Dave Milligan, I would go on to serve hundreds of people in buying and selling homes up and down the Sunshine Coast before eventually turning my attention to managing, and sharing Ryan's lessons with others.

With special thanks to, and in memory of,

Ryan Campbell

APPENDICES:

Each of the following Appendices can also be downloaded, free of charge, at www.alanstewart.ca/resources

Appendix A: Keyboard Shortcuts

WINDOWS: Top 10 Essential Keyboard Shortcuts

1. Find a word or phrase in any document or website: CTRL+F
2. Copy a selected item: Ctrl+C
3. Cut a selected item: Ctrl+X
4. Type "snipping" into the start menu to access the Snipping Tool, which will allow you to capture whatever you see on your screen into a file or the memory.
5. Paste: Ctrl+V (or WITHOUT formating in most programs: CTRL+SHIFT+V)
6. Undo an action: Ctrl+Z
7. Print: Ctrl+P
8. Switch between open windows Alt+Tab
9. Minimize the window: Windows logo key ⊞ +Down Arrow
10. Zoom in, zoom out: CTRL + Plus Sign or Minus Sign OR CTRL + scroll wheel on mouse

MAC: Top 10 Essential Keyboard Shortcuts

1. Command + Tab (toggle between programs)
2. Command + Shift + 3 (take screenshot; the default settings will save it to a predefined location, usually the "Pictures" folder and name it "Picture1," "Picture2," etc.)
3. Command + Z (undo last operation)
4. Command + Y (redo last operation)
5. Command + S (save)
6. Command + A (select all in active window; e.g., select all text on page)
7. Command + X (cut to clipboard)
8. Command + C (copy)
9. Command + V (paste)
10. Command + F (find; search for a word or phrase)

Appendix B: Goal Setting and Annual Business Plan

This goal setting worksheet is 16 pages long and can help you clearly identify how to reach your goals.

It can be downloaded at www.alanstewart.ca/resources

Appendix C: Buyer Worksheet

How long have you been looking for a home?	
What neighbourhoods are you interested in exploring?	
What is it about these neighbourhoods that makes them interesting?	*Schools, parks, proximity to work,....*
Do you have friends or family in the neighbourhood?	*Who?...*
Do you have a clear picture in your mind of what your perfect home would look like?	*Can you describe it? How many bedrooms and baths? Specific features?...*
Have you seen any specific homes that you like? Can you describe them for me?	*Pay attention to benefits over features...*

How soon would you like to move in?	
Do you need to sell an existing home to buy the next one?	
Are you working with any other Real Estate Agents in looking for a home?	*If not, may I prepare a complimentary CMA?...*
What price range are you considering? Have you been prequalified by a financial institution?	
How much are you prepared to pay monthly on your mortgage?	
How much do you intend to put towards the down payment?	

Are there any other people who need to see the home before you make a decision to buy?	
Would be ready to make an offer on a house today if we were able to find the PERFECT home for you?	*If not, why not?...*
What is the best way to reach you in the event that a suitable property comes on the market?	
Are there any other questions or concerns you have?	

Appendix D: Buyer Checklist Information Sheet

Can be downloaded at www.alanstewart.ca/resources

Buyer Checklist / Information Sheet

Source		Date	
Name (1)		Cell	☐Text OK
email		Other	
Name (2)		Cell	☐Text OK
email		Other	
Address			
Address 2			
Price Range		Move Date	
Motivation	☐ L ☐ M ☐ H ☐ URGENT!	Type	☐Detached ☐ Attached ☐ Multi ☐ Land
Pets		# Family	
Needs			
Wants			

Buyer Provided / Acknowledged	To Do Upon Accepted Offer
Agency Brochure (signed and in file)	Transaction Record Sheet
Exclusive Buyer's Agency Agreement	Offer & Deposit to Office
Home Buyer's Guide	Contract sent to lender
Current Market Information Graph	Purchaser's S.I.N.'s
Current Listings	Deposit Rec'd (copy to Listing Agent)
First Time Buyers Exemption	Mortgage Approved
RRSP Downpayment Info	Bylaws & Financials(Strata) subject removal date:
5% Downpayment Recommendation	Title, Inspection, and other subject removal date:
Mortgage Broker Referral	FINTRAC Identification
Blank Contract for review	Lawyers Names (Buyer / Seller)

Appendix E: Pre-Listing Appointment Checklist

Can be downloaded at www.alanstewart.ca/resources

Listing Checklist / Information Sheet

Listing Date			Expiry Date	
Name (1)		☐Primary	Cell	☐Text OK
email			Other	
Name (2)		☐Primary	Cell	☐Text OK
email			Other	
Property Address				
Mailing Address				
Showings				
Notes				

Compile Prior to Listing Appointment ☑

Clipboard and 2 pens	Digital Camera Kit
Tablet / Laptop	Tripod
Sample marketing material presentation	Additional memory card
Business Cards	Additional battery - charged
Agency Brochure	Tape and Bosch DLR130K Laser Measure
Pre-Printed Listing Agreement	Yard Sign with inserts
Property Condition Disclosure	Mallet and tool kit with knife and zap straps
FINTRAC ID Forms	Lock Box
CMA	Spray Paint and spray can trigger
MLS Data Input Forms	Work Gloves

To Do List During and After Listing Appointment ☑

Agency Brochure, PCDS, FINTRAC & Listing Agreement Completed	Prepare Ad Copy ☐ Client's Approved
Copy of Documents to Seller or Access to Online Folder	Prepare Feature Sheet w/ floor plan ☐ Client's Approved
Home Measurements and Floor Plan Ordered	Listing Package Provided to Office
Photos Ordered / Taken	For Sale Sign Installed ☐ Custom Rider
Obtain Keys / Lockbox Code or Key #:	Arrange Date for Agents Open:
Complete Data Input Sheet	Arrange Date for Public Open:
Taxes and Title Confirmed / Charges Ordered	Order Just Listed Postcards and distribute
Obtain Strata Plan / Lot Plan	Contact REALTORS with nearby listings
Obtain Financials and Bylaws (Strata)	Review MLS Input for any errors
Listing on Sales Board in Office	Launch Social Media Campaign

Upon Accepted Offer / Upon Firm Sale

Upon Accepted Offer	Upon Firm Sale
Transaction Record Sheet to Office	Subject Removal to Office
Contract and Deposit to Office	Buyer's Lawyer:
Deposit increase date:	Seller's Lawyer
Mortgage Approved By:	Referral Form (if applicable)
Strata Docs by date:	Install SOLD sign
Inspections by date:	Order Change of Address Cards for Sellers
Other Subjects by date:	Order Just Sold Postcards and distribute

Immediately Prior to Closing

Remove Sign	Call Clients to ensure document signing completed
Purchase closing gift	Arrange for keys to buyers and possession instructions
Meet Buyers and Agent on Possession Date	Deliver Client Gift 2 days after possession

Appendix F: Seller's Pre-Listing Checklist

Can be downloaded at www.alanstewart.ca/resources

Put on a fresh pair of glasses and try and look at your house from a potential buyer's perspective, working from the curb, through your home, and into the backyard. Imagine that you were looking to purchase a home like yours. How would your home stack up on the following? Every job on this list will add cash and result in a faster sale. Appeal to emotions to add to the bottom line results.

ENTRYWAY	Return	Done	To do	N/A
Check your front door to see if it needs painting.	$$			
Polish door fixtures if needed.	$			
Purchase a fresh welcome mat.	$$			
PAINT		Done	To do	N/A
Paint the outside of your home if needed.	$$			
Paint trim and mouldings if needed	$$$			
LANDSCAPING		Done	To do	N/A
Potted plants and flowers make your home look beautiful and tell a buyer you care	$$$			
Make sure the lawn is cut, weeds are pulled and ground covers look fresh	$$			

DECLUTTER: SHORT TERM PAIN FOR LONG TERM GAIN	Done	To do	N/A
One of the best and least expensive ways to improve the appearance and feel in your home is to clear out your closets and rooms as much as possible. Consider renting a storage locker.	$$$		
A place for everything and everything in its place. If it can't be neatly placed in a drawer or put away on a shelf, box it up.	$$$		
Organize all closets. Make sure it doesn't look like they are overflowing	$$		
Organize and clean out all cabinets and drawers.	$		
Clear all clutter from the countertops. Less is more!	$$		
Remove papers and unnecessary items.	$$		
Organize, straighten and coordinate your hanging space.	$$		
KITCHENS: YOUR HOME'S FOCAL POINT	Done	To do	N/A
Store infrequently used appliances.	$$		
Remove as much as possible from the counters.	$$		
Remove all the fridge magnets and miscellaneous hanging items	$$		
Closets and storage areas:			
Improve perception of size by removing items you aren't using.	$$$		

		Done	To do	N/A
Clean your stove inside and out.	$$$			
Clean the kitchen exhaust hood.	$$$			
Make sure your refrigerator is clean and organized.	$$$			
Clean your counters every day so they look and smell good.	$$$			
Organize the insides of your cabinets; show how much space you have.	$$			
Fresh flowers make a BIG difference for showings.	$$$			
GARAGE: THE MAN CAVE		Done	To do	N/A
Rent a storage locker for excess tools and storage.	$$$			
Consider using concrete paint to cover oil stains if necessary	$$			
GENERAL CLEANING: A SIGN OF CARE.		Done	To do	N/A
Deep Clean. Hire a cleaning service or do it yourself.	$$$			
Surface Clean for freshness before every showings.	$$$			
Have your windows cleaned, inside and out.	$$			
Dust everywhere. It's amazing how much dust you find after you move out.	$$			
FLOORING		Done	To do	N/A

		Done	To do	N/A
Refinish if necessary or clean and polish all floors.	$$			
Steam clean carpets or replace if necessary, especially if odor is an issue.	$$			
Wash all baseboards	$			

BATHROOMS: A MAKE OR BREAK POINT		Done	To do	N/A
Clean soap residue in a shower.	$$			
Purchase a new shower curtain if it is dirty.	$$$			
Clean accumulated dirt in the track of a sliding shower door.	$$			
Fix soiled or missing grout and apply silicone sealer.	$$			
Clean toilets and tighten lids or replace if necessary.	$$$			
Buy a new bath mat if it looks dirty or tired.	$$			

Appendix G: Listing Checklist

Can be downloaded at www.alanstewart.ca/resources

Listing Checklist / Information Sheet

Listing Date			Expiry Date		
Name (1)		☐Primary	Cell		☐Text OK
email			Other		
Name (2)		☐Primary	Cell		☐Text OK
email			Other		
Property Address					
Mailing Address					
Showing Instructions					

Checklist

Agency Brochure, PCDS, FINTRAC & Listing Agreement	Prepare Ad Copy ☐ Client's Approved
Copy of Documents to Seller or Access to Online Folder	Prepare Feature Sheet w/ floor plan ☐ Client's Approved
Home Measurements and Floor Plan Ordered	Listing Package Provided to Office
Photos Ordered / Taken	For Sale Sign Installed ☐ Ordered ☐ Custom Rider
Obtain Keys / Lockbox Code or Key #.	Date for Agents Open:
Complete Data Input Sheet	Date for Public Open:
Taxes and Title Confirmed / Charges Ordered	Order Just Listed Postcards and distribute
Obtain Strata Plan / Lot Plan	Contact REALTORS with nearby listings
Obtain Financials and Bylaws (Strata)	Review MLS Input for any errors
Listing on Sales Board in Office	Launch Social Media Campaign

Upon Accepted Offer / Upon Firm Sale

Upon Accepted Offer	Upon Firm Sale
Transaction Record Sheet to Office	Subject Removal to Office
Contract and Deposit to Office	Buyer's Lawyer:
Deposit increase date:	Seller's Lawyer:
Mortgage Approved By:	Referral Form (if applicable)
Strata Docs by date:	Install SOLD sign
Inspections by date:	Order Change of Address Cards for Sellers
Other Subjects by date:	Order Just Sold Postcards and distribute

Immediately Prior to Closing

Remove Sign	Call Clients to ensure document signing completed
Purchase closing gift	Arrange for keys to buyers and possession instructions
Meet Buyers and Agent on Possession Date	Deliver Client Gift 2 days after possession

Appendix H: Simple Newsletter Template

Can be downloaded at www.alanstewart.ca/resources

Median Price Graph as provided by Victoria Real Estate Board

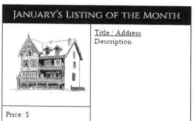

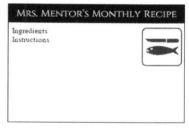

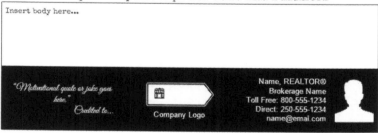

Made in the USA
Charleston, SC
29 November 2016